Summer to Fall

Notes and Numina
from the Maine Woods

Dana Wilde

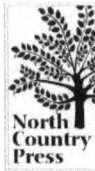

North
Country
Press

Summer to Fall

ISBN 978-1-943424-11-5
Library of Congress Control Number: 2016943958

M31 illustration on page 149 by Chris Peary

North Country Press
Unity, Maine

Acknowledgments

Most of these essays first appeared in the *Kennebec Journal* and *Morning Sentinel* newspapers' Backyard Naturalist column, in slightly or radically different versions. Some others first appeared in the *Bangor Daily News'* Amateur Naturalist column and in *The Other End of the Driveway* (Booklocker 2011). "Chebeague Island and the Tides of Time" first appeared in a slightly different version in *The Working Waterfront*. "The Auroras of Autumn" first appeared in the Barre-Montpelier (Vermont) *Times Argus*. "No Butterflies" first appeared online on the website of the Zen Fellowship of Bakersfield (California).

Preface

The most gorgeous weather in the world happens in Maine from about the middle of July to the latter part of October. Its earliest signs appear as soon as April, and its last vestiges wink away in November. In between we pay a heavy price, but this book is about the transit through the waking seasons, the flora and fauna that fill them, and the conditions of light that are ceaselessly suggesting the whole thing is much, much larger than the breathtaking sliver that's being revealed.

Part of the beauty is in the fantastic physical mechanisms science uncovers and describes. So doses of that kind of information appear most of the way through this book. When it does appear, it's spillover from the feelings of awe, desire, fear, comfort and whatever else spontaneously generates, so it seems, when you lay eyes, ears, nose on nature's configurations of summer energy. Science's own finding in the last hundred years or so is that the observer of a process is never actually separate from the process. What you see transpires in your mind, and what transpires in your mind shapes what you see. The beauty of a summer day is not a cold perception of the color blue, but your mind playing on a sea surface full of clouds.

These little essays are tries at disclosing the vortices that spin up where the sky of your mind vanishes into the sea of concrete reality. They are glimpses of divinity flaring up and vanishing. You can read them from start to finish – from the April hints to the last bare branch of November – or you can open the book and fall onto any particular chapter.

Exposing the feel of an autumn day requires a delicate verbal balance that is never precisely struck. But the exact moment when summer breaks into fall is never precisely struck in nature, either. Or at least, it can never be exactly located, given the velocity at which we're traveling through it. It is an eternally recurrent process spinning from night to day, summer to fall, dizzy with stupendous beauty.

August 2015

Table of Contents

The Return of the Juncos

One of those persistently frigid mornings in a chilly April, I heard outside the bedroom window two notes that had been absent for, well, a long time. Not quite believing my ears, I looked out and saw, sure enough, the phoebe was back, bouncing from the bare Bebb willow to the gray-birch branches and inspecting the nest up under the eaves to see what damage the winter chaos did.

Around the same time, my wife Bonnie and I were startled one evening by the clacking and clattering of Canada geese flying low over the woods. Purple martin scouts the week before were checking to see if the bird condo at the Unity park was still in orderly condition. Ducks were bringing symmetries to the air again as they bustled back and forth in twos and threes over rivers and half-frozen swamps.

Summer always returns, and the really kinetic sign of the time is the juncos.

They arrive in huge crowds every year in April and take over the yard for a day or two or sometimes a week. Their flocks are described as being as large as twenty-five, but I have to tell you, at our house they usually come in big bop-hopping droves. Juncos rooting around in leaves under the feeder. Juncos bouncing from spruceling to ground and back to spruce. Juncos exploring in the driveway like fifth-graders at recess. One birdwatcher on a birding listserve reported "bushels of juncos" at his house. The flock is a little moveable cosmos of its own.

Our dark-eyed juncos are of the slate-colored race. Junco hyemalis, they're called by the scientists, among whom there has been discussion in recent decades about what strictly constitutes a junco species, as the different slate-colored, white-winged, Oregon and gray-headed races interbreed. Anyway, they are a kind of sparrow, living in fir woods and feeding largely on seeds and, during breeding time, bugs such as wasps, moths, butterflies and even ants. They nest mainly on the ground or in the root tangles of fallen trees. I haven't actually seen a junco nest, since in our yard they're transients of April and October on their way to and from winter digs as far south as Mexico and breeding grounds as far north as Labrador. In fact they are apparently the original "snowbirds."

Junco mating behavior offers even the scientists an opportunity to talk about larger matters. One study revealed that male juncos with high levels of testosterone found their way with heightened success among many different females, so each high-T male was responsible for a lot of eggs. At the same time, the junco studs were far less attentive to the nests and chicks than the males that were less disposed to philandering, and so fewer of their offspring survived. This was interpreted – by actual scientists – as a potential moral lesson for humans.

Thoreau, who taught us to see the universe's larger spheres in the natural world, mentions the juncos here and there in his journals. But in *Walden* his principal avian sign of the time seems to be the geese: "As it grew darker," he says of one evening during the transition out of winter, "I was startled by the honking of geese flying low over the woods." They're one of spring's revelations, signifying that "the coming in of spring is like the creation of Cosmos out of Chaos." Which is exactly how, every year, the juncos come to the Middle Troy woods.

The Phoebes

The phoebes arrive with the juncos in the middle of April. They always spend a lot of time circuiting the yard, flitting from the birches and Bebb willow outside the bedroom window, darting around the side of the house among the cedars and firs, then through the sumacs, a poplar and a few birches and ashes to the open part of the yard by the garage.

One year it seemed like the phoebe couple were spending an inordinate lot of time together.

What I mean by that is, Bonnie and I got the feeling during that May and June that our two Eastern phoebes actually liked each other, which apparently is unusual for this species (Sayornis phoebe). The bird books all indicate phoebes are more or less loners who migrate by themselves or in a flock of another species, and who mate monogamously (a trait we domesticated humans imagine accords well with the moral universe we live in) but don't spend a lot of time together (which does not accord so well with our ideas of marital devotion).

The female uses moss, leaves, grass and mud to build a nest under a cliff edge or the eaves of a house. One year the nest was on the beam up inside the garage. The next year, in an interesting twist, they rebuilt on a site that had been used a few years earlier under the eave of the house just off the bathroom window. She lays six or eight eggs, the two of them tend the nest for a couple of weeks – keeping their distance from each other, the books say – the chicks fledge like thieves in the night, and then by late May or so the couple go their separate ways. Unless they have a second round of chicks, they're not seen again until next year when the same two might return and refurbish last year's homestead.

But this couple never kept their distance, that we could see. They appeared and disappeared in the birches and maples together, perching and wagging their tails down and up, and watching for wandering butterflies, dragonflies and other winged things which they attacked and snatched in mid-air. (The ornithologists call this "sallying," as opposed to "hawking" which refers to hunting bugs on the wing.) Whenever we noticed them, usually by spotting wings fluttering from the eaves or hearing the fee-bee, fee-bee song, they were flycatching along the same route, and taking brief, apparently playful runs at each other.

We interpreted these runs as more than just bird sex, which is normally quick as a wink because most male birds do not have an extending organ and the act is more like a kiss than a coupling. Young men will for the most part do it whenever they come to it, after whatever fashion suits their species, but still, these two phoebes were not kissing by the book. They were not avoiding each other.

We came to think they were in the very ecstasy of love. But what do we know? Maybe we were remembering our own lilac time, dwelling too much on what happened some years – well, face it – decades ago, and interpreting between our own experience and theirs, which is little more than a speechless drama to us. The birds do not actually tell us what's going on, or actually rejoice in the nest.

They keep house for a few brief weeks then, like spring, evaporate into summer.

What birds feel for actual emotions is unknown to us. It looks like a lot more than just brute instinct. Does last year's nest look to a phoebe, returning from distant southern lands, the same way our little log house looked to us in those adventurous years when we used to return from Shanghai and Sofia? Is home where the nest is? Or are the winter feeding grounds as close to a phoebe's heart as the eaves of a Waldo County house?

Maybe for them there is really nothing glad, nothing like our own experience back in the heyday of our own blood. But still, it looks for all the world like they're participating in that same ancient springtime madness. I think that's a fair thought to have, even if it refers to lust and nothing more. Being reasonably well-versed in country matters, I can't believe the phoebes' nest, or their pairing, is any more accidental than ours.

The Gone Robins

The phoebes and juncos return every year in a racy racket of activity. And in the midst of it, we one day, without quite knowing exactly when they started to appear, realize we have been seeing and not seeing the robins.

Seen because: Somewhere around junco time, a robin was poking around out by the Shed. Not seen because: Or was it several robins? Or was that last year? As if the phoebes and juncos were family members, while the robins barely existed.

Of course, the robins have always been there. Because of their red-brick fronts they were the easiest bird I learned to spot when I was a boy just upwind of Portland. More robin images have probably formed on my retinas than any other species of bird except possibly crows, gulls and chickadees. But because they're so familiar, I hardly even see them.

Case in point: In the middle of a recent January I was amazed to come upon what appeared to be hundreds of robins squawking, chattering and bouncing around the branches of bare hawthorn trees beside a parking lot. *What's this?* I thought, *a whole biosphere of robins in the middle of winter? I've never seen this before.*

Or check that – never noticed it. As it turns out, it's not an unheard-of phenomenon. Turdus migratorius, true to its species name, is migratory – and its range is enormous, stretching over most of North America from breeding grounds in Labrador and around Hudson Bay, down to winter digs in southern Mexico. The year-round territory extends from Canada and Maine to Southern California and Florida. They start making their way north as early as February. So robins in winter are not anomalies.

I just never noticed. You can tell from this that I'm not an excursionary bird-watcher. I mostly keep track of my own little backyard avian cosmos. Chickadees, nuthatches, phoebes, juncos in spring and fall, hummingbirds buzzing us in summer, blue jays by the task force, woodpeckers and flickers, sparrows, mourning doves, passer-by warblers, wild turkeys, the occasional owl or hawk reconnoitering for voles, once in a while a goldfinch, vireo, pheasant. Canada geese clattering along designated air traffic patterns above the treetops. Once there appeared to be an ovenbird meditating silently in the brush off the back door. Crows, of course, and sometimes a thrush.

When I say thrush, I'm picturing a wood thrush. But what I really mean, practically without knowing it, is robins. Come to think of them, they're there a lot, pulling worms out of wet earth, hopping around under the red osier dogwood, holding their chests out and their heads up on perpetual red alert. In spring they're after early bugs, but their diet, according to the guidebooks, is a mix of animal and plant, depending on what's available.

The males get here first in spring and mark out nesting territory by song. They prefer maples and spruces, it seems, and sometimes last year's nest is revamped by the female. Like most birds, they practice well-honed domestic routines. The female sits on the clutch of blue eggs, and the male guards the homestead.

After the chicks leave the nest, they stay home for a while, and the male continues to take care of them until their foraging skills are fully functional. Domestic responsibilities like this are characteristic of most birds, not to mention other creatures as diverse as cats, wolf spiders (who ride around safely on their mothers' backs after they're born), and humans.

Not surprisingly, robins operate definite communication networks invisible to us, but essential to them.

They defend their territories by mobbing – cooperatively harassing, buzzing, shouting at, and even attacking threats to the nest – and they apparently talk about strategies. Researchers have parsed from robin-speak two calls used during predator threats, "chirps" and "chucks." Robins who attacked a blue jay chirped, while others who held back and did not actually attack chucked. They used the same warnings for snakes, but at a lower frequency of vocalization. The researchers believed the robins were, indeed, communicating not just warnings, but defense strategies (to attack or not attack).

You don't really see this until you carefully look for it. But home building and protection, care for young, subrational communications all certainly look a lot like things we're all practicing together.

But it's new information about robins to me because I just haven't paid much attention to what I've already seen in abundance. And make no mistake – even though you might not notice them, robins are one of the species who have profited from human development and by all accounts are thriving. So many robins, and so little awareness on my part.

It makes you wonder what else is right before your eyes that you're not seeing. Like fish debating whether there's such a thing as an "ocean."

Signs of the Time

Every year, sometime in March or April when it's clear winter is actually going to break, I look up one evening while I'm making my way across the Arctic freeze of my driveway, and am startled to see my old friend Leo.

No matter what the cold and snow do to your mind, the sky keeps strictly to the schedule. Around 9 p.m. in the middle of April, Leo dominates my southern treetops. Which must explain at some archetypal level inside my neocortex why I am always glad to see it. And shyly behind the pines lower in the southeast, Virgo is following.

It really is getting on toward summer.

On a clear night, look south and you can pretty easily spot Leo's six brightest stars, roughly in the shape of an anvil. To the left at the narrow end is Denebola, our foreshortened version of the Arabic phrase dhanab al-asad, the lion's tail. At the lower right of the anvil is Regulus, the brightest star in Leo. In the imagination's star-lion, Regulus is at the joint of the front legs. Directly above Regulus is Eta Leonis (with no name of its own, oddly, just the Greek letter eta), in the lion's chest, and above and slightly left is Algieba (al jabbah, the mane), at the shoulder.

If you track your eye above Algieba, you'll see three more stars, not quite so bright, looping in a sort of backward question mark; these outline the lion's head. Along the lion's back, the star between Algieba and Denebola is Zosma, which sounds like a name out of some rambling fantasy trilogy and is actually a misapplied version of a Greek word for girdle. Arab astronomers more appropriately called it Al Thahr al Asad, the lion's back.

9

If you imagine the Sun traveling a great circle every year across the sky, that path – called the ecliptic – runs through the twelve constellations of the Zodiac (plus one other, Ophiuchus). Leo is one of the twelve. To its east lies Virgo. To the west is Cancer, the Crab, made of four dimmer stars.

Like all the constellations, Leo also has a lot of interesting objects that you can't see with your naked eye. But with a little help from the astronomers and their large telescopes and calculations, your mind's eye can picture them.

Some are galaxies. About a third of the way from Regulus to Denebola, and down a bit, is the Leo I group of galaxies. They're part of the Virgo Supercluster and are in the vicinity of eight hundred twenty thousand light-years from us, too faint to see without a telescope, of course. A little farther toward Denebola is the Leo Triplet group of galaxies, or M66 group, around thirty-five million light-years away.

Eta Leonis, bright in the anvil, is a supergiant star, far, far away, but so big and fiery we see it easily. The estimates vary, but it's somewhere around twenty-five times as large as the Sun and has a luminosity of five thousand six hundred suns, or some think up to nine thousand five hundred suns. Robert Burnham, whose *Celestial Handbook* has more or less scriptural authority among starwatchers, estimates it could be as luminous as thirteen thousand suns. Eta is somewhere between one thousand three hundred and one thousand eight hundred light-years away from us; if it were 32.6 light-years from us (a standard used to compare stars' brightnesses, called the absolute magnitude), it would outshine even Venus in the sky.

Southeast of Regulus is another supergiant you can see, Rho Leonis. Rho is estimated to be from three thousand six hundred and fifty to five thousand light-years away and has a luminosity of one hundred sixty-five thousand or maybe up to two hundred ninety-five thousand suns. To us it shines at magnitude 3.85, well within our naked-eye sight, but its absolute magnitude is probably around minus 5.7, even brighter than Eta.

In our backyard, much of the southern sky is walled off by evergreen trees. This has the disadvantage of blocking out a lot of stars you can otherwise see over an unobstructed horizon. But it also has the advantage of creating a frame of pointed firs that stars and constellations circulate through year after year.

Climbing into that frame behind Leo in April and May is Virgo, the Virgin. By the time she's topping the firs in mid-evening, bluets, violets and starflowers have busted out of the sudden torrent of green grass and summer is – cautiously – imminent.

The lesser main stars in Virgo are around magnitude 3, and its outline is a little irregular compared to Leo or the Big Dipper, so she does not strike your eye prominently. But you can readily find Virgo's brightest star, Spica, by looking northward to the Big Dipper and tracing from the handle a slightly angled line to the next bright star, reddish Arcturus, and continuing on that imaginary line southward to Spica, which shines pretty brightly at just about magnitude 1. (The lower the number, the brighter the star.)

Spica is a very large star – two stars, actually, orbiting within about eleven million miles of each other – two hundred and fifty light-years away. The larger of the two shines in its vicinity of space with roughly the luminosity of twelve thousand one hundred suns.

Spica is Latin for ear of wheat. The constellation figure of Virgo is holding this ear of wheat – Spica – in her left hand.

As with most star names, this picture goes far back. The Greek name was Stachys, also meaning ear of grain. The

Arabic was Sunbala, from a phrase meaning sheaf of wheat. This association of Spica with an ear of grain goes back into Babylonian and Sumerian times, more than three thousand years ago and probably further.

The ear of grain is a metaphor carrying the whole constellation's ancient association with innocence and virtue. This sense of innocence was associated, in turn, with maidenhood, and the grain metaphor came into play because depicting a human figure – particularly in Middle Eastern cultures – was forbidden. Especially, perhaps, in the divinely powerful stars. The grain also implied, quite naturally, an association with the spirit of the harvest, since later on, in autumn, Spica disappears from the sky just as the farmers are reaping the summer's crops.

If you remember your Greek mythology, you know that Demeter was the goddess of the harvest (the Romans called her Ceres – note our word "cereal"), and Demeter's daughter, Persephone, got tangled up in a dispute with Hades, the god of the underworld, which was settled by Persephone spending half the year underground with him – winter – and half the year above – summer. Spica, the ear of grain, starts to grow up in the sky again in spring, after its winterlong absence, a sign the spirit of summer is returning.

In Greek, the Horae, or Seasons, were the three sisters Dike (Justice), Eunomia (Order) and Eirene (Peace). Some Romans referred to Virgo as Pax, Peace, and around the same time the constellation was associated with Astraea, the goddess of justice, with her scales in the neighboring constellation Libra.

It seems, somehow, only fair that winter should concede to summer, a process that some springs seems to plod as almost imperceptibly forward through April and May as the constellations mounting the fir tops every evening. The Sun climbs higher. Spring grips down and awakens with a kind of innocence. The stars frame out the natural justice of the seasons. By May, Leo has crossed the driveway again like an old friend returning, then moving on. Virgo has made her way up over the evergreens again. Spica is in full star bloom up there, poised among the spike-topped trees like an inflorescence of summer grass.

Right there by the house.

Starflowers

On the edge of the fir and hemlock woods, just off the deck of the house, a little grove of starflowers springs out of the sphagnum moss and wispy grass every May. It started out some years ago as maybe a half dozen plants, and a few cycles later there were about forty scattered around under the spruce-bough eaves.

They're extraordinarily delicate-looking, with six or seven white petals in shapely points. The kind of flower that starts to make you uneasy about the idea that genetics is guided by accidents. The blossom tops a very slender stalk, one or two, sometimes three to a plant. Some guidebooks describe them as "fragile." Behind the blossom, sort of like a cosmic background, is a layered whorl of dark green leaves, lance-shaped and as rich-looking as the flower.

Starflowers are perennials. An individual will grow and blossom up to three years, or so I've read and do in part believe it, from an underearth rhizome, a stem of the plant growing underground. The petals go by in a week or so, and the leaves yellow and fall off by summer, leaving one or two little seed capsules ripening on the tip of the stem. They wait out the winter for a cold treatment, then germinate in the fall of the second year.

The scientific name is Trientalis borealis, or sometimes Trientalis americana or Lysimachia borealis. The genus name Trientalis probably derives from Latin describing the plant's height, about one-third of a foot, and borealis means northern. Lysimachia is, roughly, Latin for loosestrife, which older guidebooks give as the starflower's family. More often it's categorized in the primrose family.

14

I'm not really sure why, but I expected to find out starflowers have multiple medicinal uses, but it's not mentioned in Peterson's *Field Guide to Medicinal Plants and Herbs of Eastern and Central North America*, and a troll repeated on Internet sites is that no one's ever used it as a remedy for anything.

This turns out to be not exactly true. And the more I think about it, the further I go with it. Frank Speck, the great-grandfather of academic studies of Northeastern Native Americans, observed about a hundred years ago in *Medicine Practices of the Northeastern Algonquians* that among the Montagnais Indians, "for general sickness, and incidentally for consumption, star anemone (Trientalis americana) otseqdtuq, 'little light star', also otemdna'n kwi', 'heart berry plant', is steeped." Another researcher found that Paiute Indians used the starflower's juice as an eye treatment, and another that Ojibwas included the root in a mixture for a smoking scent to attract deer.

Anyway, I guess it's no threat to pharmaceutical company profits and won't get banned anytime soon. It's listed as endangered in Georgia and Kentucky, and as threatened in Illinois and Tennessee. In Maine it's pretty common, as far as I can tell, right in the kind of spot it's growing at our place, cool woods just on the edge of the canopy, in from the sunstruck bluets and strawberry blossoms, out from the Canada mayflowers a bit farther into the shade. The perfect place for our little grove.

We don't see ourselves making a tea out of them, but on the other hand a strong sense of evening develops out of those little stars. Always on the back end of spring, just as summer is about to drop but winter is not yet forgotten, they emerge one by one from the cosmic background radiation of new moss and infant timothy. After a long winter of consumption by cold and dark, we're breathing easy again. Just what stars dispense on still, fragrant summer evenings. This can't be accidental.

Speaking Chickadee

In our woods the easiest birds to identify who aren't crows or blue jays are the chickadees. Black-capped chickadees, they are, though more north of here you can sometimes spot the boreal chickadees, who have a brown cap on their heads instead of black.

Their songs differ, too, or so I read, since I believe I've never heard the boreal chickadee sing. They named themselves: chickadee-dee-dee, they shout from deep in our oaks, birches, maples, firs and pines. They repeat several other phrases, too, including, sort of, "seet" and "day-day-day," and a two-note tune which, with my guitar tuned by electronic device to A-440, I've measured as descending exactly a half-tone. I've heard A to A-flat, A-flat to G, and E to E-flat. You might transcribe the first note as a dotted quarter note, and every so often the second note breaks into a third.

Starting in about April and into summer, this "fee-bee" phrase gets sung a lot. According to the researchers, only males who are at some distance from the rest of the flock and from their own nests sing it. It appears to be a territorial marker, as they're sociable but feisty little birds who live together in groups of about six to twelve. It could also (imagining outward from what I've seen and heard in my own woods and books) be a communication with the mate. "Where are you?"

I can't say for sure, though. I can tell you that one June afternoon a chickadee was repeating the two-note tune nonstop for about half an hour. Imagining he was lonely, I whistled back. There was a long pause after my first whistle. Probably it sounded so goofy to the chickadee that he wondered if somebody was hurt. But then he tried again. I answered, and this time he called right back. Or so I interpreted it, and I think I was right because our whistles went back and forth as if we were conversing.

"What's he saying?" I said to Bonnie, who was digging around in plant pots on the deck.

"He either thinks you're his girlfriend or he's trying to get you to fill the feeder," she said.

"I doubt if it's the feeder," I said, because chickadees eat mainly caterpillars, bugs and spiders, and they hit the feeder mostly in winter when the bug store is depleted. They actually stock up bugs by cramming them in the cracks of trees and coming back for them later.

We whistled back and forth for ten or fifteen minutes. Eventually I thought of other things to do and wandered into the house.

In a little while Bonnie said from the deck, "I think you broke its heart."

"What do you mean?"

"After you went inside," she said, "it kept trying to get your attention. It got almost frantic, and then gave up."

Now, this could have a lot of possible meanings, because chickadee females have a tendency to, well, stray off with males they like better. I might have sounded to the chickadee cuckold like a wife who was asking to come home again. Or like another female looking for a fling.

This could all be hopeless musico-anthropomorphizing. But maybe not.

A study of their calls some years ago concluded that chickadees talk to each other about danger. The "seet" call indicates to the rest of the flock that some rapidly moving predator, like a hawk, is in the neighborhood, and to watch out. "Chick-a-dee-dee" is known to the ornithologists as a mobbing call, because it means "flock together, everybody" to harass and drive off an intruder, or at least make it harder to single out anyone in the flock. Subtle variations on chick-a-dee-dee indicate there's a stationary danger nearby, and even its size and threat level, such as that of a cat or a perched owl. Other variations convey information about food and the caller's identity.

Who the little fellow I was talking to thought I might be, I of course have no idea. But interspecies communication is not, well, unheard of. Researchers have also found that nuthatches, who forage in our woods too, appear to speak some chickadee, and understand some of the warning calls much better than I understood the two-note tune.

There is more in the chick-a-dee-dee-dees than is dreamt of in our philosophy, apparently.

Cherry May

Across the last two weeks or so of May in central Maine, spring jumps out suddenly like flowers on a shrub. In fact, the month of May is almost literally a flower. Stems and buds redden, and a sort of supernatural apparition unfolds in the woods. Several whispering shades of green emerge, and for a moment in the middle of the month those soft jades and olives flood hills and roadsides. Then, blossoms unfold.

The directest sign that the world – at least the one I live in – is teetering into that perennial delirium is the appearance of shadbush blossoms. The trees are mostly gangly branched creatures eight or ten feet high leaning after sunlight, and aren't really noticeable any other time of year. But their early leaves have a brick-red fringe and an evening-yellow duskiness, and on that background appear star-shaped white flowers of five widely spaced petals each. It's called shadbush or shadblow because its blossom time is about the same as when the shad, a kind of herring, run up rivers to spawn. It's also called juneberry, serviceberry or scientifically, Amelanchier nantucketensis, and is of the rose family.

A rose by any other name – like wild strawberry, crabapple, hawthorn or chokecherry who all throw out summer-longing flowers too – is equally sweet, but the shadbush blossoms in my lexicon stand for the first mid-May my wife and I spent together. That was true madness, it seemed to me then and every spring since, because every pastel green place I looked, I thought I saw her face, especially in the shadblossoms. Once you know what to look for, it's suddenly everywhere.

Cherry May

I still see it now. In May and June everything young becomes oblivious to everything except the way it produces itself. Nature unfolds the life force into visible shapes. The flowers of shadbush, lilacs, rhododendrons, and then the honeysuckle and every other force, appear to crystallize out of something invisible, like drops of water taking form out of the morning air on spider webs, or like time-lapse video of clouds boiling from empty sky.

The unfoldment of May has a headlong momentum of its own that gives it the feel of a living, breathing being. In ages past in Europe the whole phenomenon of spring, and in turn the motion into summer, fall and the death and dormancy of winter, was understood to be a white goddess who each year revealed herself in blossoms, especially on trees and shrubs. Not a person but an overwhelming force that crystallized out of the green and the people and everything else. For a fleeting moment around the Flower Moon there was no difference between who they loved and spring herself, and out of it came May Day and poetry.

The whole north slope of Mount Harris in Dixmont turns soft green and then, when the shadbushes blossom, unfolds into the air and sky and everywhere else.

Or so it seems to me. You live like who you are in this green. We call it simply "spring," but even when it had different names in eons past it was still the same headlong perfection of life run wild. The forces in the trees speak in flowers. The ancient ollaves and bards expressed the same forces in poetry, which (we might recall) Poe defined as "The Rhythmical Creation of Beauty." A force that you become every time it dazzles you there in the green and you say so.

Cherry May

in cherry May your hair
disturbs my equilibrium
in disproportion to
the dull of March,
the mud of April,
rain of cold acute December

sweet green buds disturb
the sunlight in the silver maples,
blur the middle distance in degrees
protracted out of angular winter

you to me are May,
coronal risk of highlights
in proportion to the clarity of snow,
the sealike foam of maple buds,
the frail refrains of June & fall,
the phrases of quadratic life

Within a Budding Grove

During that ecstatic month-long quaking of nature we call simply "June," hundreds of globeflower bushes prepare to fire up the bog off the west shore of Unity Pond.

They're called globeflowers because their little four-petal tubular white blossoms grow close together in nearly perfect spheres an inch or two in diameter, with long pistils poking out like antennae all over the surface. On a summer afternoon meander you come upon not a specimen but whole sprawling groves growing along pond sides and slow-moving streams. The creamy-white globose clusters dotting the bushes far into the distance look like thousands of buttons. A globeflower by any other name would smell as sweet: It's also called buttonbush, and scientifically Cephalanthus occidentalis, or Western headflower, of the bedstraw or madder family, and since it's a honey plant with a jasmine-like scent, it's also called honey balls.

Buttonbush is insect-pollinated (as opposed to wind-pollinated), so characteristically it has nectar to attract sweet-seeking insects. Bees nuzzle into the blossoms and brush against the flower's four stamens, which are the male parts. At the top of the stamen is the anther, which holds sacs of pollen. As the pollen ripens in the summer sunlight, the anther swells and then bursts open, releasing the pollen grains. The pollen rubs off on the bees, who move to the next blossom and rub it onto the pistil, the female part.

At the top of the pistil is the stigma, which is sticky. Once captured by that mysterious surface, a pollen grain settles in and germinates a pollen tube which penetrates the stigma and grows down into the flower's style, a slender sheath leading to the ovary. There the gametes meet. The pollen fertilizes the buttonbush's two ovules, and twins are produced in the form of little seeds that in the fall drop into the water and make their way to wet growing ground.

Among angiosperms, or flowering plants, the buttonbush globes are sweet beyond belief to the eye. You can easily think of them as little planets lighting up their green universe of shiny leaves, which are sometimes hairy underneath. Out of deep space come pollen-bearing bees stimulating the anthers and stigmas of thousands of tiny blossoms and depositing the materials of life, the way comets are thought by some astrobiologists to seed planets.

It's a natural miracle you can see performed every year, if you have the sense to look for it in the endless cycle of your afternoon strolls. Even if you can't name them when you come upon them, the jasmine scent and the sight of those ten-thousand inflorescences imitating the rotation of glowing spheres can strike like planetary madness. It's the feeling you've seen all this before in a different form, as though the shadow of your young wife is in the flowers. You remember with great clarity the sticky sweetness of summers long past. The old nickname "Honey," which you've called her for years and for your part has been appropriate enough, is doffed, and now enlightened to the true part of her, which as Juliet Capulet observed is neither hand, foot, face nor arm, you call her "Buttonbush."

What am I thinking. Nothing, actually. By now I'm completely out of my head. These are not thoughts at all but the fires of June speaking even at this time of life. Summer cools to maturity. In the freshest flower is the autumn seed. We were crazy in those days of bedstraw and budding groves.

Ancient Light

In the middle of some gorgeous June day every year, I think: "I've seen this before." It's a particular peculiar quality of clear blue light, like an apparition of summer, that turns up only in June. Certain skies in August, October and February have their music, too. But the richness and clarity of June's blue are almost supernatural.

I wonder why.

I'm sure one facet is that by June we've just emerged from winter and so the possibilities of a sunny day look very fresh. And pastel May has transformed into a sort of young adulthood: The woods are a deep green that fits like puzzle pieces into that blue sky. Maybe a quality of moisture in the atmosphere sets June's hue off from the haze of July and the shimmer of September.

There is also, most significantly maybe, the angle of the Sun. It arrows down from its highest point in June, and surely there's a slant-of-light factor, high and direct, unseen at any other time of year, that influences how the blue strikes your eye.

Because the Earth is tilted on its axis and also orbiting, the Sun appears to travel up and down the sky over the year. It reaches its highest point around June 21, and then begins to descend – in other words, every day its highest spot in the sky is a little lower than the day before. It reaches its lowest midday height around December 21. It then turns back and starts ascending again toward June. The high and low points in the sky are the solstices – a word that comes down through antiquity from the Latin "solstitium," meaning the point at which the Sun stands still. ("Sol" means Sun, and "stitium" is apparently a form of the verb "sistatum," meaning to come to a stop.)

The farther north you are, the more the Sun's altitude in the sky varies, and so does the length of daylight. Central Maine occupies territory just about halfway between the equator and the pole, so our summer days are noticeably much longer than our winter days. Once I spent June and July in northern England, 10 more degrees of latitude farther north than Troy, and was dazed by the fact that "midnight's all a glimmer" in reality – it never gets fully dark there in high summer. Still farther north the Sun never sets at all around the summer solstice, and never rises in the December time. (In the Southern Hemisphere, the cycle is the exact reverse – in June is the winter solstice, and the summer solstice occurs in December.)

When June's blue strikes here in Maine, I come every year into the disquieting recollection that people have been tracking this up and down path of the Sun for three thousand years, and more. How long before?

The oldest written record of astronomical calculations is a catalog from Babylon of risings of Venus over twenty-one years about 1600 B.C. The Sky Disk of Nebra, Germany, is also about three thousand six hundred years old and has a patina inlaid with a gold Sun, crescent phases of the Moon, and thirty-two stars in a dome, showing the Pleiades, Ursa Major and Eridanus as seen in the sky at the time. But it seems clear that a detailed knowledge of sky motions goes back centuries further, probably a lot further. The Great Pyramids of Egypt, which are thought to have been built in the centuries around 2700 B.C., show signs of orientation to the stars. Stonehenge, which is thought to have been first built at roughly the same time as the pyramids, has standing stones arranged to indicate the exact times of solstices.

And there's reason to believe sky motions were being tracked even before the pyramids or Stonehenge were built. A site dated to around 5000 B.C. at Goseck, Germany, consists of concentric ditches and palisade rings with gates aligned to sunrise and sunset at the solstices. This implies people were closely tracking the sun and stars at least seven thousand years ago. How long before they built such facilities were they making observations?

In their book *Hamlet's Mill*, MIT professor Giorgio de Santillana and Hertha von Dechend contended that all of world mythology is a coded oral record of astronomical information. The stories behind the constellations – Taurus (the bull), Leo (the lion), Hercules (the hero), for example – are the late, remaining versions of some of these stories. Hamlet comes into the picture in a story of a grinding mill that falls into the ocean and a hero named Amlodi that is told in one version in the Finnish story cycle *Kalevala;* de Santillana says this story depicts an ancient knowledge of the precession of the equinoxes, in which the pole star changes position over a regular cycle of about twenty-six thousand years. The ancient skywatchers did not know that the Earth is tilted on its axis, and wobbling, causing the stars to appear to make a stupendous slow-motion circuit of the sky. But they apparently were well aware that the stars change position over millennia, like giant cosmic wheels grinding time to dust, and that the Sun travels a regular path every year, and they told stories figuratively detailing their knowledge of these awesome motions.

If this is true, the implications are astounding. It means the original stories could be fifty thousand years old – probably older. This is not hard to believe, if you ask me. It seems likely that full-blown language, with the capacity for abstraction, was being spoken at least seventy thousand years ago, and probably earlier. If so, then people were telling stories around campfires, and the sky in its awesome, ever-changing yet ever-stable expanse would have been a matter of fascination, description and discussion.

The Sun is the most prominent celestial body, and so it would take no more than a few years for even one perceptive person living in the Earth's middle latitudes to notice that it travels up and down the sky, corresponding to warm and cold, growing and withering seasons. If such people encoded and passed along this knowledge in stories, then the myth of the gods of the waxing and waning year, as the poet Robert Graves phrases it, is beyond ancient.

Maybe the June blue is not just a seasonal configuration of greenery, atmospheric moisture and high angles of light. Maybe my eye transports the same sense of ancient immanence as the distant ancestors who watched the mysterious and all-powerful Sun appear and disappear. We can't really understand, in any rational way, how they thought or what they knew. In their philosophy, dreams sparked by starlight were as real and important as summer and growing trees.

And there it is, it seems, right in your eye, deep in the blue, blue sky of June.

Midsummer

Suddenly, it's midsummer.

Late afternoon, a great blue heron with crooked neck and slow-motion wingbeat cruises across the park in Unity. Purple martins nesting in the bird condos by the baseball field dart around like point-winged aerobats and poke their gatherings into the holes where little heads peer out. Passers-by too close to the kids for martin comfort get buzzed, birds veering down at heads.

On the road a goldfinch plays chicken between a car and a pickup truck. In the backyard, a robin launches from under the sumac and flaps into the cedars. A squad of blue jays scolds something in the hemlocks.

The first goldenrod of the year appears in a field. Meadowsweet, with conical arrays of blossoms beautiful in the afternoon heat. Dust-pink steeplebush. A lone orange poppy pokes its head up out of the weeds beside the driveway, and down the embankment is the last of the yearly spray of day lilies. White clover waist-high. A field of fireweed. Cat-tails. Tough little pineapple weed growing in gravel, sweet-smelling when they're cut. Purple nightshade creeping out from under the chokecherry bush.

A tangle of wild madder, with tiny white stars for flowers and green whorls for leaves, is crowding around a post of the porch. Queen Anne's lace umbels hover like white moons suspended in space.

Hercules is overhead after dusk, a trapezoid of stars with four limbs shooting off the joints. In a clear sky and a pair of binoculars you can spot a hazy ball of light between two of the stars, it's globular cluster M13. Southward, Altair burns over the fir tops in Aquila, the Eagle, and up and to the left is even brighter Vega, which will shift slowly northward as the millennia pass and eventually become the pole star. Meanwhile the seven bright stars of Ursa Major are up there circling around Polaris, the north star for now.

Trying to piece together how long flowers have graced the Earth (the first blossoms appeared about one hundred forty million years ago), a strange statement by a university scientist: "People become so obsessed with flowers it is important to remember a flower is nothing more than a cluster of spore-bearing leaves surrounded by whorls of protective and often albeit attractive leaves." The point? Beauty is an illusion.

I can't believe it. On the road home, huge clouds boil up out of the sunset sky in billows and shocks of startling definition, sharp gray, purple, blue and silver shadows layered on layers. I slow down to look. In my lane another car slows, and one has pulled over. We all see it. It is not an illusion. Those giant clouds are intimidating, awesome, gorgeous.

The beauty of midsummer is as real as a living being.

Hummingbirds

We do not understand much about virtue, as Socrates often observed. But one thing we know for sure is that size has nothing to do with toughness.

Take the ruby-throated hummingbird, for example, which could be hovering by your flowers like a fine-tuned helicopter any summer day. It's about three and a half inches long. It weighs about a tenth of an ounce. Its wings span barely four inches. Its eggs are the size of peas. It eats by poking its beak into blossoms and licking out sweet nectar a drop at a time.

A drop at a time – its tiny grooved tongue flicks twelve times a second. While it hovers, its wings beat eighty times a second. Its heart – an indicator of its metabolism, which is the second-highest among warm-blooded vertebrates (only shrews are more wired) – beats about six hundred times a minute, and can double when the bird is really exerting itself. A hummingbird takes about two hundred and fifty breaths a minute. (Humans take about twelve.) It has to eat about every ten minutes to survive in good health.

These numbers have the sound of precision biodelicacy. Large dragonflies have been known to eat hummingbirds. So have spiders, quick-witted cats, and the odd kestrel streaking out of the sky toward the flowers.

But these are unusual catches – in fact, hummingbirds have few persistent enemies, and this is due at least in part to their nimbleness (hummingbirds are the only birds that can fly backward) and their alertness. They're fiercely territorial, and mark off careful boundaries in the trees which they defend like warriors.

But also, they are just physically tough. Hummingbirds can fly up to fifty miles an hour (barn swallows, the reddish-bellied air acrobats, fly about twenty miles an hour), and during spring courtship rituals the males swing and dive in great showy pendulums, beating their wings up to two hundred times a second.

Most remarkable, and instructive, is the annual migration.

Ruby-throats (Archilochus colubris) are the only hummingbirds that nest east of the Rocky Mountains. They arrive in Maine around the beginning of May (the males get here first, the females a week or two later), and set up camp for the summer. In early fall they start stuffing themselves, partly with the nectar of the remaining wildflowers, partly with insects, and sometimes with tree sap from holes drilled by yellow-bellied sapsuckers.

For what is about to happen is one of nature's amazing feats of endurance: The tiny hummingbirds, departing Maine at the end of September with stored-up energy, fly not just south, but on across the Gulf of Mexico, covering up to six hundred twenty miles nonstop.

The resilient ones make it to their winter homes in Central America. The average ruby-throat may accomplish this feat for four or five years. Some durable hummingbird elders have lived to be twelve.

I like our two cats, who skillfully keep mice from infesting the walls and squirrels from chewing up the logs of the house. But despite their eight-pound heft, they're fat, lazy, mollycoddled Romans with an easy morning's ride compared to the one-tenth-ounce hummingbirds, who maneuver like Black Hawk helicopter pilots around the dangers of the woods all summer and then fly the emptiness of Gulf space to Mexico. Now, that's tough.

The Survival of the Cormorants

In a past life I seem to remember on Casco Bay, there was a bird the fishermen called shag, and they disliked it. For my part I remember thinking the shag were kind of cool when they were arrowing in straight lines a few feet above the water in fighter-jet formations.

They were less cool when they were swimming because it seemed like they could barely float. The water washed up over the base of their necks, and they held their orange beaks up the way you hold your face when you're learning to dog-paddle. They looked like a low-rider seagull-duck. Seagulls to me were idiots, and it was years before duck beauty dawned on me.

I still kind of think seagulls are idiots, but even then I didn't believe they deserved death. My eleven-year-old mind was shocked one sunlit afternoon when I was gazing from a wharf on Mackerel Cove at Bailey Island and saw a fisherman cruise up in his outboard beside a hapless floating gull and kill it with a bait pick, like a Cossack mowing down a peasant. Feathers went everywhere and he buzzed away and left the gull crumpled and bleeding on the water.

Even then, gulls were government-protected, I think, though it didn't matter to some fishermen, who it turned out thought the gulls and especially the shag, or cormorants as I eventually learned to call them, threatened their livelihood by eating too many fish.

Settlers in New England, thinking their survival was at stake, set about early on to get rid of double-crested cormorants. By the early 1800s the birds had been extirpated from our region. But they have a huge range in the world, and by the 1920s they were documented to be nesting again in Maine. The fishing industry saw them as such a threat that in the 1940s and '50s oil was systematically sprayed on some one hundred eighty-eight thousand eggs to get rid of them. It didn't really work.

By the mid-1960s a number of harvestable fish species were noticeably declining, and studies showed the cormorants were at least eating a lot of Atlantic salmon hatchery smolts and interfering with the new restoration project. Double-crested cormorants were shot by the hundreds.

In 1972 they came under federal protection, and their numbers increased through the turn of the present century. Whether the cormorants have a significant impact on populations of harvestable wild fish has not been established, though the common wisdom among many fishermen seems to be they do. But they still ate too many salmon smolts in the 1980s, according to studies, and with populations increasing through the 1990s, federal money made its way Down East-ward in 2004 for more studies to figure out how to deter them without having to kill them. Firecrackers, lasers and shooing them away from smolt-run areas seemed to work in one experiment on the Narraguagus River in 2004 and 2005.

Different species of cormorants live in lake and ocean areas all over the world. In our parts we see mostly double-breasted cormorants and from time to time great cormorants, which are coast dwellers. The double-crested cormorant has an orange throat pouch, and the great cormorant has a white neck patch. They dive from the surface to catch fish, and their featherage absorbs water for ballast to keep them down. After a round of fishing, they perch clumsily on a rock outcrop or a buoy and spread their waterlogged wings to dry.

As a kid I thought they were cool again when they dove. They stayed down for what seemed like impossible periods of time, popping up feet and yards from where they disappeared. Decades later, they pop into sight again, silent squadrons of two or three angling along with Doppler-like precision a few feet over the Penobscot River. They vibrate some living thread between here and boyhood. The cormorants are still fishing hereabouts, even though they're so hungry they get in the way. We're all just surviving.

The Invisible Whip-poor-wills

The whip-poor-wills used to drive me mad at night when I was a kid. Or lull me to sleep. I can't remember anything in between, it was so long ago. In bed I heard them repeat their name over and over in the dark, relentlessly, one phrase: Whip-poor-*will*. Whip-poor-*will*. Whip-poor-*will*. Whip-poor-*will*. Whip-poor-*will*. Whip-poor-*will*. Whip-poor-*will*.

It's a three-note song. In poetic meter, three syllables pronounced together in this pattern are called a cretic, or amphimacer – an unstressed syllable between two stressed syllables. (English lends itself to iambs – two-syllable patterns of one unstressed and then one stressed. The word "ago" is iambic. The iamb is the unit in that famous but tortuously enigmatic English-class phrase, "iambic pentameter.") The whip-poor-will's cretic song is unforgettable. When I called up an audio file of it from the Internet, it sounded exactly as I remember from summer nights decades ago near the coast of southern Maine.

But I can't remember hearing a whip-poor-will since then. Part of the reason, obviously, is that I spent much of the 1970s and '80s living in brick-and-pavement Portland, where whip-poor-wills don't go. They live in woods near open fields, and lay their eggs directly on the ground, usually among leaves. The birds and eggs are so intricately camouflaged they're practically invisible. The city compared to the woods and fields is bug-free, while whip-poor-wills make their living snatching insects out of the dusk in their huge maws, like their cousins the nighthawks.

I've never actually seen a whip-poor-will. But when they're there, they jar the night loud and clear. One researcher counted a whip-poor-will sing its name a thousand eighty-eight times in a row. That was long after it had been named "vociferus" (genus Caprimulgus).

But when I escaped the expansion of Portland and moved to Waldo County, I still heard no whip-poor-wills. What is going on?

The short answer is: No one knows for sure. But a National Audubon Society study reported that whip-poor-wills are one of twenty common birds (including also evening grosbeaks, chickadees, grackles, meadowlarks and several kinds of sparrows) whose numbers have declined by as much as half in the last four decades. The researchers theorize that suburban sprawl, climate change and invasive species are reshaping whip-poor-will habitat. The Massachusetts Audubon Society set about a survey a few years ago to try to find out what's happened to them – they've all but disappeared down there.

Here in Maine whip-poor-wills can still be heard. Or at least, I've heard that people have heard them. I don't know. Even stranger than the long, strange trip from the nightjar summer evenings of southern Maine to Troy, is how clear the whip-poor-wills echo in memory. As if the meter and pitch are burned permanently onto the disk. I'd give almost anything to be driven mad by that song again.

Cyanocitta cristata

The blue jays, unlike the whip-poor-wills, are loud and visible and always going somewhere. Where that is, no one knows, exactly.

They swoop in from noplace in squalls of five or ten or more and take up positions like commandos in the spruces, shouting warnings and orders the whole time.

Then one after another they raid the bird feeder outside the kitchen door. The homebodies who think they own the feeder, mostly chickadees and nuthatches, keep their distance while the big, blue, crested rangers knock seeds onto the deck and hop down to inspect their work, striding around and twisting their heads up, down and sideways like robots, watching for the cat they know must be nearby. They're so brassy they steal morsels from the cat's dish if they think it's safe.

After a while they disappear into the woods. They often seem to head west, though this is probably just a quirk of our local topography. If so, maybe there's a path through here, like an airborne deer trail. It's hard to tell if any stay in the area, the way their cousins the crows do, who stake out a territory and settle into it. In our yard at least, wave after blue wave seem to just forage on in parts unknown. All winter long the blue jays are coming, again and again, but studies show some of them migrate too. No one knows which ones or why.

It is known that blue jays are omnivorous. They eat insects, the occasional mouse or frog, and sometimes even an egg though their reputation as nest raiders is mainly unwarranted. At least three-quarters of their food is fruits and nuts, especially acorns, which they bury deep against the frost for later. Fifty Midwestern blue jays were surveilled one autumn caching a hundred and fifty thousand acorns in twenty-eight days.

They appear to have excellent memories for where they bury nuts, and in another study they seemed outright crafty about it: Their behavior was so erratic that the scientists got the feeling the blue jays knew they were being watched and deliberately scrambled their work patterns.

So much for the phrase "dumb animal." The blue jays are tricksters who know what they're doing, and also what they're talking about. Their raucous screech means "Fear! Foes!" in just one of their dialects. They also make a low whistling sound, and a noise that's been described as a growl, though to me it's more like a whine, almost catbird-like. Sometimes they whimper like a red-shouldered hawk. They're like living panpipes, echoing sounds heard in these woods long before people wandered through.

A blue jay on the wing can't be mistaken for a hawk, though. Blue jays fly like overloaded freight trains. They seem to flap ten times to get the same thrust a hawk would get in two smooth strokes. Maybe some of them give up on the idea of migrating because flying is more work than foraging.

I wonder where they're going. In Native American stories they sometimes fly up to the Moon and take part in high-level celestial shenanigans, often acting as pathfinders or figuring out how to survive a run of bad luck. This seems plausible to me. The blue jays seem to understand the sky trails and wherever between here, there and back again they lead to, even though we have no idea.

Home with the Nuthatches

Usually when the bully blue jays are off on some foray in parts unknown, the birds that bop around the feeder most frequently who are not chickadees, are the nuthatches. Red-breasted nuthatches almost exclusively, though once in a while a white-breasted nuthatch shows up, which is slightly larger and, well, has a white breast instead of a rusty-colored breast.

The red-breasted nuthatches (Sitta canadensis) seem much more serious about what they're doing than the black-capped chickadees. The chickadees flit and hop, take pokes at each other, and chatter in their polyphonogrammatic chickadee language.

The nuthatches, on the other hand, talk less and spend much of their tree time upside down. They patrol high, low and around tree trunks for beetles, ants, caterpillars and spiders, with their heads pointing mostly toward the ground and their long, sharp, flat claws finding toeholds in the cracks of the bark. In winter when bugs and spiders are scarce, they grab seeds out of the feeder.

They're quick to join other species of birds on food-finding expeditions. But their bird feeder etiquette is quite a bit more refined than the chickadees' and blue jays', who often turn up in gangs and take turns stabbing at the tray with their beaks and sending seeds flying all over everywhere. The nuthatches are usually alone, or maybe with one companion. After spending some time inspecting the tray by walking all over it upside down and sideways as though gravity didn't exist, they normally take one seed at a time with their longer beaks and, like the chickadees, fly off to hammer it open at another location. A study done deep in the Franklin County woods some years ago showed that nuthatches and chickadees both select seeds according to weight, indicating they're aware that the heavier seeds contain more nut meat.

The nuthatches are on the whole less talkative than the chickadees, although they apparently study chickadee language in school because they understand the warning calls. Their own vocabulary has a lot of variations on a call that sounds roughly like "yank-yank-yank," sort of a nasal cross between a crow and a duck, but tiny; a series of rapid "hn-hn-hn" notes; and a trill that apparently occurs at mating time, which I have not noticed myself.

Nuthatches seem to live in small groups of two or three birds; researchers have noted male pairs living together in the same small territory. The males are said to be aggressively protective of their nests, especially while the female is building it, though I've never observed this either. In fact the nuthatches seem to me to conduct themselves with a sort of domestic calm-headedness, compared to the other flying residents of our woods. Being small, high-metabolism creatures, they do bustle around with jerky movements, but even their sharp motion seems more deliberate than the garrulous chickadees. They're methodical, but not officious. Vigilant, but not skittish.

Their whole demeanor looks to me like they have, on the whole, an energetic but more serious disposition to hearth and home. They excavate holes in dead branches where they make their nests of grass, bark and pine needles, and they paint the openings with pine or spruce pitch – using their beaks or (reportedly) even a piece of bark as an applicator – whose stickiness is thought to keep predators from coming in. (Which explains why we see them so frequently: Our woods are thick with spruce and fir.)

I imagine chickadees, by the feisty way they move around and chatter, have a better sense of humor than nuthatches. But their females are prone to have affairs, which is not observed among the nuthatches, who are seasonally monogamous. During the courtship phase, the male brings tasty caterpillars and bugs to the female and places them in her bill with his, and if the off-season foraging is good, nuthatch pairs will overwinter together and nest again the next spring. When winter foraging is particularly bad, nuthatches will up and head south en masse in irruptions.

Here in Troy, they're at the feeder all year round, so the domestic arrangements must be suiting their homespun little dispositions.

Why the Barred Owl Sings

Long ago when I was really a sub-novice bird-watcher (unlike recent years, when the best you can say is that birds fascinate me and I recognize a few shapes, feathers and calls), I was walking around in the Vermont woods early one morning with a bunch of actual birders. They pointed out a redstart, a few warblers whose names I instantly forgot, and a turkey vulture. Somewhere in the middle distance a rhythmic hooting sounded that even I could tell was coming from an owl.

"It's a bard owl!" one of them said.

Bard owl, I thought. That's a cool name for a bird whose call sounds hauntingly poetic to begin with.

"I wonder what play he's quoting from," I said. They all looked at me blankly, like I was out of my mind. Well, no matter, it's happened before, and no one's ever held a grudge against my verbal incomprehensibilities. That I know of, anyway.

Years later, I was reading about owls in Maine because we were hearing one at night in the woods of Middle Troy. Hooo hooo hoo-hooooo.

Great horned owl. Northern saw-whet owl. Long-eared owl. Short-eared owl. Barred owl. Eastern screech owl.

Wait a minute. "Barred" owl?

So this bird I registered as Shakespeare's colleague was not a bard at all, but barred. Funny thing about sounds.

If you listen carefully to the musical phrases, there's a difference between "bard owl" and "barred owl." "Bard owl" is a phrase you'd tend to pronounce with stress on the first word and less stress on the second – BARD owl. In poetics

43

(which *is* within my field of expertise), this unit of rhythm is called a trochee. This is what the birders in Vermont were articulating.

What they thought they were saying, however, was "barred owl," which in everyday American speech would normally be pronounced with roughly the same stress on both words – BARRED OWL. This stress pattern is called, technically, a spondee. In barred owl, most of us might let the second word fall off almost imperceptibly, reducing the distance between what the two phrases sound like, and mean – bard and barred. But the difference is negligible if you're not listening for it.

These probably seem like irritatingly minute distinctions to most people, and some will scan the phrases differently. But the truth is, sounds carry profound meaning even in the fine details. Poetry, in one way of saying it, is language articulated at a level of musicality between everyday speech and singing. In the right conditions, speech can erupt into poetry at any moment. A shift in stress can mean the difference between a bird along the driveway and Shakespeare.

The barred owl (Strix varia) we heard calling in our woods was likely to be the same one we heard the year before, during the lunar eclipse. Barred owls do not migrate, according to the ornithologists, and have not been observed to travel more than six miles from areas where they've been studied. They live in forests of mixed trees, like ours, often near water, and prey on animals that are pretty abundant here, such as squirrels (overabundant, frankly), chipmunks, mice, other birds, frogs, toads, even fish, bugs and worms. They tear the heads off the larger animals and eat them first, and they're known to stash leftovers in trees. They fare badly in neighborhoods with great horned owls, who prey on them and their eggs, and on the other hand are a similar problem to spotted owls out west, where they've been encroaching in the past century.

The barred owl song that haunts our woods at night is usually transliterated into English as "Who cooks for you? Who cooks for you-all?", with an extra syllable dropping from the end of the echoing line. In poetics, that falling-off stress at the end is called a feminine ending. One study sorted out six distinct barred owl vocalizations, including a variation on the nine-syllable song with ascending, more uniform stresses; "duets" of calls and responses between two birds; "a two-syllable 'hoo-aw'"; "a one-syllable, sharply ascending wail"; and "an irregular and patternless assemblage of hoots," described by other observers as chaotic screaming.

We don't know what goes through the calling bird's mind. Or the effect of the call on the bird that hears it. It's not random babble, though, which implies the owls understand what the fine details in the sounds mean. A long time ago some birders in Massachusetts used a whistle to elicit replies from a barred owl, and discovered the pitch of the replies was B-natural. A later formal study determined female barred owls call at a higher pitch than males. Song is the owl's everyday speech.

Their primordial lines of poetry have been sung in these woods for who knows how many millennia, 11,000 years at least, going by fossil records. Hooo hooo hoo-hooooo, hooo hooo hoo-hooooo-aww. An echoing ghostlike gorgeousness, like the sound of an eclipse. It has Shakespearean depth, gravid with the kinds of meaning singing produces, even when you don't know the language.

The birders in Vermont articulated it exactly accurately.

Food for Thought

"What kind of grass is that?" Bonnie said, waving her hand toward the tall purplish-topped fronds beside the walk in the Unity park.

I couldn't answer because I didn't know any more than she did. Though maybe I should have, because every so often in the summer I set out to learn how to identify the grasses in these parts, breaking out books, searching online and foraying in fields.

But it might as well be hieroglyphics. There are just too many kinds of grass, with too many similarities of stem, flower and structure – fourteen hundred species north of Mexico and eleven thousand or more worldwide (scientific family Poaceae, aka Gramineae) – to learn in your spare time and do anything else with your life.

I can pick out timothy and redtop, the way I can pick out the Chinese characters for "man" and "learn." But most of the rest is a wild babel. Around here there's calamus (aka sweetflag), foxtail, orchard grass, purpletop, plantains, ryes, witch grass, switchgrass, crabgrass, bluegrass, beach grass (aka Ammophila breviligulata), and hundreds of others I can't identify for certain or pronounce.

And that's just grasses, as distinguished from sedges, rushes and cattails – though telling a grass from a sedge is not much more difficult than telling one foreign language from another. Even if you don't speak them, German and Russian can be distinguished by sound, and grasses and sedges can be distinguished by sight. Grasses have hollow, jointed stems that are usually round. Sedges have solid stems and no joints. Rushes have solid stems and flowers resembling lilies. Grass has flowers, too, they're just not colorful. The sprays on a grass plant are the blossoms. Unlike other plants' flowers, the inflorescences on grasses remain long after the plant has seeded and gone by.

After family resemblances, though, grass vocabulary passes my understanding. During a couple of summers I grew grouchy about my inability to find my specimens in the books, but my disposition got better after I realized this is not something you learn easily. Three summers later I narrowed down that tall, beautiful, purple-topped rhetoric in the park: It's reed canary grass. With instruction I could have understood it sooner. Someday someone will tell me what kind of grass grows in the bog by the Kanokolus boat launch, and I'll memorize it, like an ideogram.

This ignorance about grasses is startling, given the fact that we live on them. Corn, wheat and rice are grasses – and practically everyone who ever lived in the past ten thousand years ate at least one of them in quantity. So is sugar cane. So are the oats in your breakfast gruel. The barley in your beer. The bamboo shoots in your curry.

Luckily for us, grass grows practically everywhere on and into earth – as much as ninety percent of a grass plant is underground. One study showed that a four-month-old greenhouse-grown rye plant had three hundred eighty-seven miles of roots.

There really is no word for these kinds of depth and complexity. Grass has been growing for at least fifty-eight million years, according to agrostologists who have studied grass fossils. This is roughly fifty-seven million years longer than human beings have had speech, if the ability to make a campfire implies that language existed to preserve technological knowledge.

I wonder who first turned a campfire into an oven and wheat into bread. Generations upon generations of people have come and gone just in the ten thousand years since farming started. Man does not live by grass alone, but how many grains of corn, wheat and rice have been transformed into flesh, blood, brains and thoughts by how many human bodies?

Whether grass turns into words by luck or by design, I don't know. At some point I hope some great universal naturalist will teach me the name of the grass that clothes the bog in summer green so I can tell it to Bonnie, who could tell it to our son Jack, who could tell it to his as-yet unsprouted kids, who no doubt also will be bread eaters. On and on. This whole process is different from what anyone ever supposed, and luckier.

An Ancient Moment

In July there's a sort of pause in the dash to fall. A slowdown, like rounding a bend in the pavement. It doesn't last long, maybe five minutes when you're looking out over a new-mown hayfield, or maybe a week or two if you can get hold of it in your mind and watch.

It's pretty much seamless – August and September are right around the corner – but it's right there, closer than you think. Goldenrod and Queen Anne's lace appear magically along the edge of fields. Steeplebush blossoms arise like dust-pink mirror images of meadowsweet. Uncut grass turning brown in the mid-July Sun. Lake water lapping on the shore at dusk.

Morning unveils on blue jays and doves overrunning the feeders at our small log house. Honeybees loud in the roses. Goldfinch wingbeats. Sumac blossoms like little Christmas trees. Ants and especially slugs have population booms sometimes in mid-July; walking from the driveway to the porch it's almost impossible not to squash them. White admiral butterflies – jet black with white trim – skip around the driveway, the big yellow and black Eastern swallowtails, and white tail dragonflies, large, beautiful and ferocious.

Cobwebs get built in the shed windows and cabled from bookshelf to bookshelf; dead wings dangle in them like paper kites. A house spider tends an egg sac suspended in its web on the back of a lawn chair where my own son sits sometimes in summer.

When I stand in the driveway, the early-born and long-lived-evening daylight of July seems eternally paused. But it's slipping toward autumn, now. We won't see this length of light again until next May.

Which is a way of saying the whole moment is in a state of ever-present returning. The ancient forest is always everywhere around us, no matter what we think we're doing.

About dusk one quiet late July evening an awful retching bark came out of the woods just a few feet from the deck. Then rending, slavering, snorting sounds and a terrified peep-peeping erupted and went on for it seemed like forever. What must have been a fox was killing what must have been a turkey. It was close and invisible. The ancient forest is right there. Despite chain saws, rented cars, pavement and space stations, you can feel it, frightening and going full bore in this gigantic midsummer pause that is, in scientific fact, eternity.

Yellow Alchemy

True story.

On an expanse of mown grass in Unity one summer, I glanced down, caught a glint of yellow in the green, and bent down to look. A low, creeping plant with roundish, shallowly lobed leaves had escaped being leveled by lawn machinery. It had small blossoms with green petals and a dusty gold center disk. *No idea what this is*, I thought, and broke off a piece to check with the wildflower books. Long chapter short, I looked and looked but couldn't find it.

Every spring the green ones come again from the other world in supernatural abundance and start their mercurial transformations, and the anchoring color of the whole process from spring to fall is yellow – the glint in that unknown flower. A lot of eruptions crack the earth open in March and April, but the first full-blown sign of life is the forsythia. After that all heaven breaks loose. Dandelions strike full force about the first of May with a tipsy cheerfulness hardly to be believed. By June the hawkweeds are in it too, and all kinds of buttercups. Even bluets are golden at the core.

Patches of roadside turn bright yellow with birdsfoot trefoil and hop clover. The tiny heads of least hop clover pop out, and then the petal-less, greenish pineapple weed masquerading in scent as chamomile. Clumps of St. Johnswort, unkempt in the distance but neat up close, back the ditches, and everywhere are black-eyed Susans in an intense state of yellow that's already started the journey along the spectrum to orange, and to what will be the red and gold of autumn.

By midsummer, while cow vetch and fireweed, Queen Anne's lace and ox-eye daisies are lighting up the day, the color yellow is channeling sunlight everywhere: Goldfinches and sulphur butterflies haunt the brush; yellow wood sorrel with little cloverlike leaves shows its face through veils of grass; toadflax, or butter-and-eggs, in places you'd think plants can't grow; and on field edges, cinquefoils with petals so precisely carved they look like some divinity handcrafted them. Venus, maybe, after she used the silvery dusk to unfurl evening primrose blossoms. Pale yellow, pale the primrose, the light changes and moves away.

When low-angled afternoon light filters through green leaves, in the translucence you can see yellow is transforming the world green. Ballfield grass by July is tinged with that pervasive sulfur hue, while the next generation of summer emerges restlessly out of the copper earth: Goldenrod to me is the emblem of the transformation to maturity. Where there isn't goldenrod there are groves of wild parsnip. Sow thistle like raggedy dandelions. Yellow goatsbeard in tall grass. Fringed loosestrife and swamp candles half-hidden in wet grassy spots. Mullein by the railroad tracks, and the little blossoms of gangly black mustard. Tansy for all of us, buttonlike disks.

Summer culminates in sunflowers, as though the whole green world was preparing all along to break open in those huge blossoms. Their heads bend toward the Sun from morning to night, as if every day was an ecstatic rite of worship. On their watch, the red giant arrives and turns maple leaves Martian orange, birch leaves yellow, and ripens golden apples in the Sun.

All this was visible back in July if you knew how to look at it. The fleabane and daisies have gold in their disks like sunflower harbingers, not to mention that unknown plant in

Unity. A few days after I spotted it, I was walking across my rough-hewn lawn in a sort of silvery, moony state of consciousness when the word "saxifrage" came into my head. Where it came from, I don't know. It was as if rock cracked open and the word appeared like a glint from another world.

What does "saxifrage" mean? Is it even a real word, or is it something J.R.R. Tolkien might have made up, like "elanor" or "evermind"? No, it seemed like a real word, and I wondered if it might be a flower. It sounds like a flower name.

I got out the wildflower book. In the index was the word "saxifrage," yes. The picture showed a creeping plant with roundish, shallowly lobed leaves, small green blossoms and a reddish-gold center.

The flower in Unity was golden saxifrage. If your eye can find it, the ore is everywhere. In my case, I need more grace than I thought.

The Day of the Trefoils

In late July, somewhat unbelievably, summer starts making its cosmic pivot out of highlong Sun toward blackshadow August and full, gold autumn.

Suddenly the grass has topped out and gone to seed. Like a blind-sideways blow, the supernatural green explosion of May and June has already turned into twinkles of meadowsweet.

First daisies, cow vetch and buttercups crept in like stars emerging out of twilight, fleabane like multiple-sun systems on green stalks overseeing it all. The apparition of hawkweed faces in crowds, like a neater make of dandelion. Yarrow, bedstraw, water hemlock (fatal), and field groves of three-umbeled pastel valerian. Big tangles of lavender-blue crown vetch.

Suddenly all kinds of three-leaf clovers, white, red, hop and rabbit-foot, appear as if they fell out of the sky. The dust-pink cascades of milkweed blossoms open up. Stitchwort, like galaxies on tendrils in the talling grass, acts like a psychedelic drug on the mind errant. This all happens by the middle of July.

Sometimes the really blinding weed of hot summer is the birdsfoot trefoil. Little tripartite lip-flowers that grow in yellow crowds near pavement and fences. Lotus corniculatis, the botanists call them. How the genus "Lotus" got there, I don't know. The guides say they were introduced from Europe, but I think their origins were further out, somewhere the other side of the Buddhist pure lands. This is the kind of flower, who, after you stare at a patch long enough, you swear has come from outer space.

Maybe it all did. Some astrobiologists think life on Earth began when comets sprayed in through the atmosphere carrying chemicals believed to be the precursors of sentient beings. Amino acids – organic molecules basic to the chemistry of life – have been found on plenty of meteorites, and experiments have shown that linked pairs of them (dipeptides) are chemically viable in outer space conditions, and could have ridden to Earth on comet dust and catalyzed proteins, enzymes and sugars into life.

It's less far-fetched than it sounds. Some scientists say a meteorite that crashed onto Sri Lanka in 2012 has algae fossils, and arguments have been made that microscopic fossils are embedded in meteorites that were blasted off Mars millions of years ago and later fell to Earth in Antarctica and Egypt.

Panspermia, the theory is called, that suggests life is being pervasively distributed throughout the universe on comets and other traveling chunks of rock and ice.

I don't know, of course. I only know that the bright yellow birdsfoot trefoil along the roadside at the Unity park, when seen in a certain slant of mind, has an otherworldly glow that stings the inner eye and opens up a momentary conduit connecting flower blossom to places like the Trifid nebula, where stars are spinning up out of clouds of dust and appearing in deep space the way flowers spin up in grass and carry starlight into the edge of midsummer.

Stars and Flowers

Call me crazy, but I can't get the similarity of flowers to stars out of my mind.

Under the trees at the edge of my yard appears a blossom every spring that looks so much like a twinkling star that its common name is starflower. Daisies, sunflowers and black-eyed Susans are also stars by etymology: They're all "asters," Latin for star, because their petals fan out like twinkling starlight.

Now, stars do not actually throw out individual rays. They radiate light more or less uniformly through space, the way the Sun does. But stars are so far away – from a few to millions of light-years – that their light spreads out through space, diminishes in brightness, and finally gets bent and refracted in the Earth's atmosphere into what looks like twinkling. In binoculars or a camera lens, spikes or rays seem to dance off the edge of each spot of light. Closely grouped stars blur together, like in clusters and galaxies that appear to be single spots but are millions or billions of individual stars, each with its own rays blending into the others.

A lot of flower blossoms are no bigger than a star is to your eye, like the wild madder and other bedstraws. They grow in fields on tangles of stems that are virtually invisible from a distance, and their tiny four-rayed blossoms, less than a quarter-inch wide, are packed together in small clusters, like little Pleiades or Hyades. They almost twinkle there in the grass. The wild madder blossoms are so numerous and close they strike your eye like roadside galaxies – billions of stars like a cloud.

The tiny white flowers on chokecherry bushes unify into tubelike sprays, or racemes, from a distance. The disks, or umbels, of Queen Anne's lace are made of scores of tiny blossoms in the shape of elliptical galaxies, and they grow suspended over fields in groups, like Hubble Space Telescope images of the edge of infinity.

One night I dreamed about stitchwort blossoms. I am not making this up.

The stitchwort flowers are white stars, half an inch or so across, of five petals so deeply cleft they look like ten. Their genus name is Stellaria. They spread out along tendrils in tall grass like spray from the Milky Way. In the dream I was trudging along the edge of a field. Magnified stitchwort blossoms appeared and disappeared in the grass. Soon there were dozens, thousands, ten thousand thousand, and I was seeing each individual flower and all of them together. Then for some unknown length of dream time, which is different from waking time, the flowers were stars, and my sleep, whatever sleep it was by then, became troubled and mixed up between outer space and the edge of the field.

Now, a flower is not a star even when it's called aster or Stellaria. But at some point which is probably at some proximity to madness, where we should never go, they seem to cross paths. I don't think I'm out of my mind. But who knows?

Stars appearing so tiny and cold, yet in reality being so enormous and hot, it sort of makes you wonder what you're actually seeing there in the magnified madder and stitchwort.

Of Goldenrod and Galaxies

Asters start appearing everywhere in August hereabouts and go well into fall.

The biggest and brightest are the sunflowers, leaning east to west from morning to night and soaking up sunlight with big yellow-gold wheels that look for all the world like stars, which is the source of the family name, Asteracea. Latin *aster*, which comes from Greek αστηρ, means "star." By September fields of stars are growing everywhere. Daisies, hawkweed, black-eyed Susans, powder blue chicory, violet blue New York asters, panicled asters, bushy fleabane, and small-flowered white asters.

•

And then there's the goldenrod, at least one hundred thirty different kinds, cascades of yellow among bushes and tangles of blue and violet stars. Rough-stemmed goldenrod grows in every field from July to October, and also seaside goldenrod, blue-stemmed, stiff, downy, tall. The flowers are close-packed on the stems and seem to be overflowing rather than sunning. But goldenrods are asters too – the cascades are made of tiny yellow blossoms that themselves are stars.

Long ago goldenrod got badmouthed for causing hay fever, but it doesn't – ragweed's the culprit. Its green flowers spill pollen the same time goldenrod blossoms. In fact, by age-old tradition goldenrod leaves make a tea you can drink for medicinal purposes, sore throat and such.

Every autumn, in the gold September light, they seem more and more gorgeous to me. At a certain point they become intoxicating. It's just me, I guess, my own taste in flowers. But they seem to march in ragged clusters up and down hillsides, bright yellow in the Sun and ageless. Whole sections of fields get flooded with gold, like sprays of the Milky Way washing through late-summer constellations. The goldenrod blossoms are close-packed stars, and it's hard not to think of them as small galaxies growing on the edge of the woods by the house. They cascade into the sunlit dry grass and asters. Like the galaxies spiraling outward in the great, dark star fields.

•

The astronomer Johannes Kepler noticed around 1600 that flower parts grow in spirals, too. Botanists call it spiral phyllotaxis, and have shown that leaves on a stem or the structures inside a seed tend to form at a particular angle to each other, which is about 137.5 degrees. That angle was well-known to ancient mathematicians and artists. Whether anyone noticed it in flowers before Kepler is uncertain, but it had a name: the golden ratio. It was understood to be a fundamental pattern of beauty in nature and art.

The golden ratio underlies the structure of pine cones, sunflower seeds and shellfish, Leonardo da Vinci's paintings and the Parthenon. It's in the spiral arms of distant collections of stars, too. Somehow your eye imbibes it, and in late summer it wheels and dances in your mind like a kaleidoscope of goldenrod, sunflowers and other asters.

Butterflies

In the 1970s, if you had told me I'd be writing about butterflies in the 2010s, I would have scoffed – one of our principal pastimes back in the Ironic Age.

But the butterflies. Most summers we have a steady population of white admirals darting around the yard between dragonflies. These white admirals are deep black with a white band on their wings. When you catch one resting you can also see dark red dots at the bottom, under the band. The sharp symmetry of the wings and their satin markings strikes the eye with a sort of planetary force. It's hard to avoid the idea that some kind of planning governs these forms.

My Lepidoptera identification skills are still in their infancy, but we get viceroys, sulphurs, azures, a red admiral or two and possibly a monarch most summers, along with all kinds of moths as well as skippers. Butterflies, skippers and moths are distinguished mainly by their antennae: Butterfly antennae are swollen at the tip; skippers' are "hooked"; and moths' are "feathery or threadlike," according to one field guide. In general butterflies are active during the day and moths at night, though there are exceptions. Most butterflies hold their wings upright when perched, while moths fold them over their backs.

These details are a lot more interesting to me now than when I was a kid. Butterflies weren't my hobby, but I remember being curious about their colors and their breeze-born erratic flight. My childhood – weird as it was, to my recollection, with maps on the evening news showing what parts of the East Coast could be destroyed by Castro's missiles (the circles reached almost to Portland) – was marked by the kaleidoscopic, almost stupefying sense that beauty was endlessly boiling up out of the natural world. I did not call it "beauty," of course, because to a nine-year-old it's not a thought, it's an experience, like the first thing you see when you wake up in the morning. Everything seemed alive, I remember. Beyond butterflies, there were stars in inky blackness, hay fields, painted turtles. The smell of cut grass could create a momentary trancelike state. My mother's hollyhocks fascinated and annoyed me, like bees. I spent parts of many summer days between about 1962 and 1966 hypnotized by the glitter of sunlight on ocean waves.

That was then. Sometime around 1967 or '68 I awoke to a sort of dejected cynicism in which the natural world retreated, like images in the wrong end of binoculars. The news from Vietnam was horrific. Kids I knew were rumored to have stolen their family cars. It was impossible to tell what was real from what was fake. Nobody loved us, or more importantly, me. All good writers were ironic, I figured out, which indicated how I should shape my own ambitions, and how thought could and should eradicate emotion. (In fact, in retrospect it appears I took all emotions for inferior, dangerous kinds of thought.) Something about wanting to get high. The world was a smothering, soporific weight. It was all downhill from there, like they say, sunglints and all.

By college, the word "aesthetic" took on a certain philosophic meaning, but the idea that a white admiral's markings sprang from any *design* would have met with skeptical dismissal from us. God, if he exists, does not work like that, we would have said with phenomenological confidence and gone on to the next topic. Which might have been the superiority of John Berryman's poetry to Robert Frost's because it gave an unvarnished depiction of real inner life. A butterfly was an emblem of sentimental weakness. Berryman jumped off a bridge in 1972.

One hot August afternoon when I was twenty-five after a bad day at work, I stopped my car in Scarborough at a roadside stand that sold cut flowers. You left a quarter in a rusty coffee can and took a bunch. I did not know much about flowers then, but there were asters among them. I brought them home thinking my roommates would appreciate them and put them in a glass of water on the kitchen table.

Then something unbelievable happened. The flowers made me feel better. It was as if the blossoms themselves were cheerful, like the ingredients of a restorative broth. My gray matter, shockingly, was transformed by that cheer.

Cheerfulness not being one of my often-mentioned traits, the mood lasted only that evening. But I carried around the image long after the flowers were no more. You might say it was all uphill from there – steep and rocky, but upward nonetheless.

In the last two or three decades, the child who was hypnotized by glittering waves has had progressively more to say to the man. Hayfields are mesmerizing again. The meanest hawkweed bending in the wind can transfix me in the yard for minutes extended and warped almost to the limit of my wife's patience. I dream stitchwort flowers are field galaxies, and am not sure afterward if I dreamed of the stitchwort or the stitchwort was dreaming of me. Stars, like some cats and dogs, almost speak.

And the butterflies. The symmetry of their wings, their black, white, orange, blue, red and yellow markings. They transform from crawling things, apparently by design, into prisms that channel some glinting radiance too deep for thought or tears or any other expressible feeling. It's like

waking up. As if the golden age, somehow, is making a
breeze-born return.

Myrmidons in Troy

Under two sumac trees near our house in Troy, a metropolis is constructed every summer. From about June through August, it gets bigger and bigger, one doorway after another appearing out of the dirt, until it spans two yards or more from city limit to city limit.

The residents bustle around hauling loads of dirt and exploring every inch of land to find out what use can be made of it. There's no technology. West across the lawn are other metropolises, somewhat smaller. They're as busy and strange as any ancient Aegean cities must have been.

Myriads of black field ants live in them. Between blades of grass and under strawberry leaves, in patches of gravel and up the trunks of ash trees, ants are everywhere, working.

The main city under the sumacs has roughly the same ground plan as ant nests everywhere. Nicely shaped conical entrances of sand frame doorways, from which tunnels descend a foot or more underground. Horizontal chambers house offspring and store food, tended by specialized workers who all know their duties.

These black field ants are foragers, raiding out to the edge of the known world and into civilized places like the house where fighting them off is usually a losing battle. They sneak in unseen, despoil the countertops of crumbs and the floor of meat bits dropped by the cats, then zigzag home. How many get lost on the return, I don't know.

In warmer parts of the Western Hemisphere there are ants that are farmers rather than raiders. Leafcutting ants strip leaves from plants, chop them up and haul the cuttings into special underground chambers to mulch fields where they grow fungi. They eat the juicy fungi tips.

Some ants, like the red fire ants that have colonized Mount Desert Island and points northeast in recent years, keep aphids the way people keep cows. They shepherd and protect the aphids, and milk them for food.

Ants, like humans, are called by myrmecologists "social animals" because they live together cooperatively. How they do this, having such tiny nerve centers for brains and (as far as anyone knows) no language, is one of nature's astonishing phenomena. The eminent entomologist E.O. Wilson once said that ants "are among the pinnacles of social evolution on this Earth." Their level of cooperation is so highly refined it's called "eusocial."

All these words mean, really, is that ants work together, like humans do. (And like humans they work together to fight ferocious battles, too, though I've never seen one, only scuffles when one ant tries to steal a morsel out of another's jaws.)

Without language per se, ants may communicate with chemical signals called pheromones which mark food trails or signal alarm. No one has yet found an ant library containing the blueprint for a nest, but somehow they share knowledge of how to build, forage and farm. What they say to each other and how they say it is further from our rational reach even than the daily life of ancient Knossos.

And yet, Knossos like the ant cities had no electricity, no calculators, no engines, but talked about how to build walls and systems of agriculture and food processing. It was a cooperative project – computers, condominiums and ant colonies result from many minds and hands working like one.

One day about three thousand five hundred years ago a huge volcanic explosion on the Aegean island of Thera (called

Santorini when I stood on its precipices thirty-some years ago – and called who knows what when the Argives and Myrmidons set out on a pretext to raid Asia Minor) destroyed Knossos, just to its south. What the residents said as the ash and smoke rained down is now out of hearing.

I wonder what the ants think when periodically during the summer a tremendous roaring and the odor of oil approach the city, and then wailing wind and a massive spinning monster shear off the conical entrances, slash the vegetation, and destroy the top layers of the city.

It doesn't matter. The ants all set to work immediately, carrying out boulders of sand and piling them neatly on the surface, recarving caved-in chambers, scooping up eggs to save the babies. They all know what to do, and do it together. And their siege on our house in Troy continues, undeterred.

Bug Love

The Argives and Myrmidons who sacked ancient Troy were motivated by the abduction of their most beautiful woman, whom they meant to retrieve. But this is not what motivates the ants and bugs who invade the house in the summer. Normally you don't even register insects in thoughts of Eros. I mean, we by and large associate love with beauty – Helen was Aphrodite's favorite – and bugs are ugly.

But despite their unspeakably violent hunting, plundering and devouring, a major part of bugs' adult lives is spent reproducing. A lot of them copulate, which could really bring some non-erotic imagery to mind, and even that can go pretty badly for the males of some species. Some female mantids eat the mate after the act, or even during. You have to want it pretty bad to dive into that.

Yet for us, like them I guess, love comes in at the eye, or some perceptor. "Only God, my dear, can love you for yourself alone, and not your yellow hair," or some such poetic nonsense. And once the physical expressions of love settle down, reality sets in, and by that I mean: offspring.

Children live a series of completely different lives, some of whose pains and joys you might remember firsthand – or be reminded of by your own offspring. The human transformations take place from toddlerhood to kidhood, from kidhood to adolescence, and finally, most radically, to adulthood. Hopefully. It's not their growing bodies that undergo the most turbulence – though there's enough, no doubt – but it's their inner, invisible, emotional lives metamorphosing from one stage to the next and turning some of them utterly unrecognizable: child, teen, adult.

Anyway, I got curious about bug love and its consequences recently when I caught two beetles in a highly suggestive pose on (appropriately enough) a wild rose blossom, thorns and all. They turned out to be blister beetles, and they were indeed engaged in the love function. Or whatever it is to them.

Adult blister beetles, like a lot of creatures, copulate, and at the beginning of the process engage in foreplay. I missed the erotic preliminaries for these two. But for up to an hour, they move about while perched atop food plants, and rub each other with their antennae or palps (fingerlike appendages near the mouth). When ready, they copulate for up to four hours rear-mount style, like a lot of other six-, four- and two-legged beasts. The female then lays fifty to several hundred eggs in dirt crevices, under stones, or sometimes on the plants, including notably clover and alfalfa. This normally happens in mid to late summer.

The eggs hatch out in around two weeks, and then things start to get bizarre. Most insects metamorphose through three or four stages of life (egg, larva, adult; or egg, larva, pupa, adult), and each stage can be unrecognizable as the same species, let alone the same individual. These blister beetles, though, don't just metamorphose–they hypermetamorphose.

This means they go through not one or two phases, or instars, after hatching, but six or seven, depending on their species and location. The first larval instar is a small item, practically all tail with legs and an antlike face (at least, so it appears in the entomologists' drawings). It attaches itself to a bee and travels off to find food, which in our area is mainly grasshopper eggs. After gorging itself, it starts developing through three or four more larval stages (collectively known by entomologists as "first grub"), in each of which its legs get smaller and its body gets bigger and blockier. When it reaches the last of the first grub instars, it's pretty much legless. These phases take about four weeks.

This grub, practically immobile, digs a hole. It metamorphoses into its second grub phase and then pupates into a kind of curled up creep (not a technical term) with folded appendages. If food sources are unfavorable for the pupa, it can retro-molt back to the first grub instar, wait out the winter and re-emerge to pupate again the next summer. (I know some parents have wished this could happen with teenagers. But this is an anomaly of bug physiology, not of human psychology.) Finally, it becomes an adult and sets about eating plants, including potatoes, and reproducing repeatedly during its one- to four-month adult life (varying according to species and conditions).

They're called blister beetles because when tampered with, the adults exude from their leg joints a chemical called cantharidin that can raise a pretty nasty-looking blister on your skin. In fact cantharidin is so toxic that a big enough belt of it incidentally ingested from beetles patrolling alfalfa or clover can kill horses.

It also has another kind of bizarre application. Cantharidin is the active ingredient in an aphrodisiac sometimes called Spanish fly, named after the European species of blister beetle it's extracted from. Now, Spanish fly does apparently work for men. In a way. Cantharidin is quite a strong irritant, and so as it travels through the urinary tract, it can increase blood flow to the nether organs and induce, well, priapism. By all accounts, it is not particularly pleasant, and can, in extreme conditions, kill you.

You have to want it pretty bad to dive into that. I don't think golden-haired Aphrodite or her offspring, or their instars, are associated with it. Speaking as a human, I mean, with a capacity to intuit a teenager from an adult, and to catch at least glimpses of supernatural beauty that you might aspire to blossom into yourself, someday.

Nursery Web

The spiders that cause probably more agonistic language on Bonnie's part around our house than any other arachnid or bug are the nursery web spiders.

I keep telling her their name should actually endear them to her because her number one criterion for evaluating the moral character of everything from bacteria to presidents is how they treat their kids. In this respect, nursery web spiders show high moral character. They get their name from the fact that for a while the female carries her egg sac around and, when the time arrives, builds a silk web where the eggs hatch, and she then guards the spiderlings for a week or so after they're born. Anthropomorphically speaking, it's kind of lovable.

The trouble is, among the six hundred and eighty or so spider species known to live in Maine, the nursery web spiders are – not to put too fine a point on it – large. Front leg tip to rear leg tip extended can span upwards of an inch, which looks like a monster to an unsuspecting dishwasher who's suddenly face to face with one on a window screen. They're hunters, so they roam around brush and sometimes the porch or other startling spots like the kitchen counter, looking for fat arthropods.

Our common species of nursery web spider in Maine, Pisaurina mira, in the universal process that leads up to the egg sac, practices a remarkable courtship and mating process – though its cousin in Europe, Pisaura mirabilis, has a unique approach that P. mira, by virtually all accounts, does not share.

Among North American, or "nearctic" P. mira, the male wanders around until he detects the silk dragline of a female. He then follows the silk, pausing cautiously for short periods and raising one of his front legs. As long as she keeps watching, he slowly approaches, and the pauses become longer. At some point the female might decide she doesn't like him, and she runs off to some inaccessible spot.

If she decides she likes him, though, she allows him close enough to gently touch her hind legs with his front legs. After some leg interplay, she scoots to an apparently predetermined mating spot, where she attaches a dragline. He quickly follows her and takes up a position behind and over her. She then dangles freely there, and he follows. Using his palps – which are the little handlike appendages spiders have beside their mouths – he carefully turns her over. While he's doing this, he folds her legs in and binds them with a "veil of silk," as one team of researchers put it.

Cradling her in his legs, he then positions himself so he can reach around her body with his palps, where his sperm is stored. With his left palp, he gently places sperm into her epigynum opening. He then repositions and repeats the insertion with his right palp.

This happens a few times until the female gets restless. He then releases her, just adding a little more binding to the veil and then retreating to a safe distance. The female, still dangling, frees herself from the silken bonds. Soon she'll be carrying around an egg sac in her palps and jaws (or chelicerae).

Very few spider species are known to bind the female with silk during copulation, but it's an at least superficially understandable practice because in many spiders, the female is apt to eat the male at some point before, during or after sex. It doesn't happen very often in most spiders, but sometimes.

So the male's binding practice is at least partly insurance against being attacked and consumed.

The European, or "palearctic" cousin takes a different approach to the whole affair. P. mirabilis is one of only a very few spider species in which the male courts the female with an offering of food.

The male, which as in most spiders is smaller than the female, usually first catches a bug, such as a fly, and usually wraps it in silk. (Giftless males in studies were by far less successful in mating than gift-bearing males.) He then locates the dragline of a female who might be willing, and carefully approaches her, holding the nuptial gift (technical phrase) in his chelicerae. If the female decides to receive him, she moves slowly toward him. He then raises the gift in his palps and leans backward. At some point, the female grabs the gift.

Occasionally she makes off with it without copulating, but usually the male maintains a grip on the gift with his legs and a line of silk. When he positions himself over her back, keeping a hold on the gift with the silk line and a leg claw is crucial for him, as we'll see in a moment, and it turns out rounder gifts are easier for him to handle than oblong gifts, which get in the way. While she's eating, he commences the reach-around copulation with his palps. The longer she keeps eating, the longer copulation lasts and the more sperm can be transferred and thus increase the number of offspring.

Sometimes the female interrupts the copulation. When this happens, the whole session might end with the male making a hasty retreat. He might also play dead, which the arachnologists call "thanatosis"; it's probably a strategy to prolong copulation, though it's not known for sure, but it very likely helps him avoid being eaten himself.

Among nursery web spiders, sexual cannibalism, as it's called, happens only about 2 to 4 percent of the time and almost always before copulation, which accounts at least partly for the males' ginger approach. But it's been known to happen afterward, and researchers observed one nursery web male eaten during copulation. He had brought no gift.

Why female spiders eat the males sometimes, the scientists aren't sure. There is some kind of awareness in little arachnid minds that enables them to choose between potential mates. But why they can be overcome by a desire to eat a mate, no one really knows.

I'm not sure how cannibalism practices play in Bonnie's existentialist philosophy of arachnid life. When I told her about all this, she just swore and said, "Of course they do that. They're *spiders*."

I think I'm in love.

Ancient Predators

Prehistoric monsters terrorize the airspace around the dooryard all summer. They have ferocious teeth. They're in the upper tiers of the food chain. They're hungry. And they're everywhere.

Luckily, they don't eat humans. Also, they're only an inch or two long – the colorful winged helicopters that dart through the air from June to about mid-September: dragonflies.

When you notice them flitting nimbly around your yard, you're watching a scene from before the dinosaurs. Dragonflies are one of the oldest species still living direct from their origins. While the first dinosaur fossils are about two hundred forty million years old, the earliest remains of a dragonfly date to about three hundred twenty million years ago. (Humans, in roughly the form we understand ourselves, have been around about two million years.)

Some of those early dragonflies had two-foot wingspans, which means they were monstrous even to human-size creatures. While the dinosaurs disappeared around sixty-five million years ago, possibly in cataclysmic climate changes after an asteroid or other piece of space debris crashed into the Earth, dragonflies continued to flourish at scaled-back sizes.

To us nowadays they're aerobatic miniatures, but they're still howling monsters to the mosquitoes, gnats and flies they eat. Dragonflies can't walk, only perch; they catch their food by arranging their spiny legs to form a sort of net. Among the most superb fliers in nature, they dart around snaring small insects, and eat on the fly, tearing off chunks of bug meat with teeth that might seem nightmarish to a mosquito, if the mosquito could think about it. Their teeth are so prominent a feature that naturalists used the Greek word for tooth, "odonto-," as the basis for the name of their scientific order, Odonata. Other people just call them mosquito hawks.

The ancient dragonflies have about five thousand species of descendants, about four hundred fifty of which inhabit North America. There actually are two main kinds of dragonflies, told apart fairly easily: the dragonflies, which are the heftier, often colorful ones, and the damselflies, which have slimmer abdomens. The dragonflies come in families such as darners (the large, brilliant blue and green ones), clubtails (with expanded tail ends), and skimmers (with patterned wings and more squat bodies), all of which, with others, are commonly seen in Maine. One thriving South American species of dragonfly has a seven-inch wingspan.

Dragonflies spend only a brief month or two flying around as adults. In the earlier stage of their life, they are six-legged bugs. They jet around in water and wait for food to stray near their mouths. This "naiad" stage can last two or three years before they metamorphose into four-winged creatures who spend one short summer netting gnats, and mating. When you see two dragonflies joined at one or both ends, they're probably engaged in the bug-erotica you almost can't help but imagine.

When dragonflies and damselflies seem to be buzzing you at your picnic table, don't worry. The darners don't really sew up your lips if you tell a lie. They're not after you, but looking with their thousands-lensed eyes for mosquitoes, who *are* after you. Like the descendants of the first working helicopter – which Igor Sikorsky shaped after them – the dragonflies are just patrolling, as they've done for three hundred million years.

Amazing Grace

One summer we were not seeing as many dragonflies as we usually do. I found this a little disconcerting for two reasons – because we depend on them to clear the air of bloodsucking flying things, and because of their amazing grace. They're like aerobatic glimpses of another whole world right before your eyes.

Maybe a cold spell or a glut of predators killed more larvae than usual that year down at the brook, which is the nearest water around our house in the woods where dragonflies are likely to breed. Or maybe that June was too rainy and cloudy, as dragonflies are solar-powered and can't do much on overcast days. I didn't really know. I missed seeing them.

As July wore on, though, their numbers started to increase, particularly the common whitetails, which are the large dark-colored skimmers that we see most. Petaltails, darners, clubtails and emeralds are some other families of dragonflies, as distinct from damselflies, which are the thin-tailed, streamlined-looking ones. Dragonflies and damselflies make up the order Odonata.

Anyway, every summer they mill around the yard like tiny helicopters snatching flies, gnats, mosquitoes and sometimes each other directly out of the air with several kinds of lightning quickness. They have a sort of lower lip that shoots out and hauls flies into their toothed maws to be torn apart. Most dragonflies can't walk, only perch, but they fly like they invented it. Their four wings beat independently of each other, not only flapping but twisting like propellers so they can stop, hover, start and make 90-degree corners in any direction with remarkable suddenness.

They can't hear. But truly amazing is their eyesight.

Most of a dragonfly's head is made up of its eyes, of which there are actually five: three tiny simple eyes on top that probably gauge light intensity, and two large alien-looking bulbs that see almost everything around it except directly behind and directly underneath. A perched dragonfly's head and eyes will twitch as it watches what's going on. And what it's seeing is different in at least four ways from what we see.

First, a dragonfly eye is made up of facets (called ommotidia), which ours aren't. Each large eye has ten thousand to thirty thousand of these hexagonal facets, each of which collects light and creates an image. Those images are compiled in a kind of flicker effect into mosaic-like picture-perceptions.

Second, dragonflies see colors we don't see. Our eyes detect only a tiny part of all the light there is. We humans have three color-receptor proteins called opsins, which detect red, green and blue wavelengths of light and form those in millions of shades. Dragonflies have four or five opsins that pick up colors beyond blue. Like other insects such as bees, dragonflies can see into the ultraviolet wavelengths of light, where our eyes cannot go.

Third, dragonflies can sort out light angles, which we can't do. What does this mean. Light waves travel at angles that are vertical, horizontal and otherwise to our eyes. The human eye receives all the angles in roughly the same way, which limits the clarity of our perception to some extent; you notice that limitation in glare. Polarizing sunglasses cut glare to your eyes by filtering out the horizontal rays of light and letting in only the vertical rays. Dragonflies, though, have the ability of polarotaxis, which means their many-faceted eyes sort the angles of light. This apparently helps them judge surfaces and distances (though they can mistake shiny surfaces like pavement, car roofs or oil slicks for water).

Fourth, dragonflies have a spot on their eyes called a fovea, which is a dense cluster of ommotidia cells that sharpens the images of what they see, especially the blue and ultraviolet colors. Humans, who see very well as creature eyesight goes, also have a fovea, but our eyes are not facet-based, so the fovea's effect is different for us.

So what do dragonflies see? The flicker effect gives them a keen sense of motion so they can locate and grab flying insects with startling precision. Their polarotaxic ability reveals to them a sky that to us is just a glare, but to them is a bright background that they can navigate by. The colors they see that we don't are reflecting off flowers, leaves and water; two black-eyed Susans that look exactly the same to us have varied color patterns to the dragonfly. Their thousands of facets pick up, not just what's in front of them, but all around them within a yard or so.

Their little odonate minds are glimpsing moment by moment snapshots of a world that we are right in the middle of, but don't see.

So when they were not showing up in the yard one June, I admit I felt a little lost. Was blind, as it were, but now thankfully can see them.

The Time of the Assassin Bugs

This is the time of the assassin bugs. In fact, all summer long is the time when everything small vigorously engages in a life of unspeakable violence, which up here in the human world we take for horror and cruelty, but on the next stage of biological size down is just, well, things as they are. It is a place that is apparently, as far as I can imagine it anyway, literally beyond good and evil.

If you could shrink to the size of dragonflies, ants, yellowjackets and sow bugs, not to mention spiders, and still have the wherewithal to think like a human, you would find yourself in a nightmare. Multifaceted yellowjacket eyes and saw-toothed mantid maws bigger than your head, and the cold, remorseless, kindless, treacherous intent there behind them.

"Treacherous" is a human idea, though. The insects are just hungry. A praying mantis will eat its brother. One July afternoon I found a bright green Zelus luridus nymph – the intermediate stage in the life cycle of the assassin bug – motionless on the side of the house near a spider's sheetweb. I assumed this meant luridus was hunting escapees from the web, or possibly the spider itself. It would seize whatever living thing its size that it found, such as an aphid, in its sticky forelegs, hold it vise-like, stab it with its beak and suck out the insides. This is not cruelty, it's just making a living.

The house spider with its nearby web was no more treacherous than a fisherman with a weir net. But what if you were the spider's size? You might wander into a tangle of sticky rope you couldn't twist, shake or pry off your arms – like the ant-mimic bee who I once watched writhe and flail in a few strands of silk for nearly half an hour. Imagine if you could think about those silk chains. Eventually the spider would run along the web and loom over you with its hairy mouth, eight glossy eyes and upthrust knees. Then it sticks you with its side-to-side jaws (or chelicerae, as the arachnologists call them from a safe distance) and injects a toxin. You're paralyzed.

Maybe you're still groggily aware of what's happening. The spider turns you around and around, coiling length after length of sticky rope over your legs, arms, chest and face. You're suffocating, it stinks and you can't move. It drags you along a silk bridge to the center of the web. There you hang, immobile, maybe you have a horrible headache and nausea. You wait. After a sick drunken eternity the spider returns, prods your silk wrapper a few times with the claws of its front legs, then with its face, and then suddenly it tears open your side, injects a fluid that turns your insides to mush, and sucks it all out.

And in this underworld spiders aren't even the top of the food chain. They're hunted by spider wasps. When a breeding female spots a wolf spider, she pounces and stings it, paralyzing it. She then drags it – alive – to a suitable hiding place in the grass or dirt, and sets to work digging a hole. This can take a half-hour or more. When the hole meets her standards, she retrieves the paralyzed spider and drags it in backward. She then lays an egg on it. In a few days the egg hatches, and the larva emerges and eats the spider alive.

Violence, science, elegance! This has been going on for hundreds of millions of years.

Thank goodness we grew big. The same way the night sky seems awesomely beautiful and familiar, the twitching eyes of a dragonfly, the swollen red glare of a house fly, the lidless gaze of a snake can on the other hand freeze your young blood. Those ancient images of horror and beauty seem to live in our minds like genetic ghosts from the evolutionary past, when something with the hallucinatory face of a crab spider blotted the morning Sun from the cave entrance. The fear of it is like a poison that's stayed in the veins of memory, as it were, and catches up the conscience.

Imagine, after we were human, the level-headed intoxication it took to stare those faces down.

The assassin bugs are alive and well on their small stage down there, beyond evil and good.

Spider Bites

My son, Jack, got annoyed with me over lunch one afternoon about black widow spiders.

He was explaining that black widows – everyone's favorite phrase to evoke arachnid peril – live in Maine. I said, well, not exactly. But he said he'd read online that you can encounter them in Maine. There was no antidote for his fears.

Had he seen some new report? As far as I understood at the time, while black widows are sometimes spotted here, they don't live here permanently because they can't survive our fatally cold winters. A bunch of them turned up in some crates at Bath Iron Works in 2011 and caused a stir of popular trepidation, but that apparently blew over. They all froze to death, no doubt.

Black widow spiders are in the same family of arachnids – Theridiidae, or comb-footed spiders – as the common house spiders that are probably spinning cobwebs in your basement. They're roughly the same shape, with big butts and relatively long legs. The house spider's technical name is Achaearanea tepidariorum (or Parasteatoda tepidariorum), and they're not the least bit dangerous to humans (except possibly in virtually unknown cases of allergic reaction).

The widow spiders are a different genus of comb-foot, Latrodectus. They're identifiable by a red hourglass marking on their underside, which is a duller color among L. geometricus, the brown widow, and brighter red among L. mactans, the Southern black widow. They live mainly in the South because they're not adapted to survive in cold weather. They are, as common wisdom holds, dangerously poisonous to humans.

Most spiders' side-to-side jaws, or chelicerae, have little fangs on the tips that can deliver venom to paralyze a victim (and then turn the insides into mush that the spider sucks out). Most spiders' little jaws are capable of biting people, but hardly any of them have fangs big enough to even notice, let alone venom strong enough to affect your system.

Most of the bites people – even doctors – attribute to spiders are probably not from spiders at all, according to the arachnologists. Often simple skin infections are mistaken for spider bites. And a lot of insects you didn't even know were there can raise a welt, including fleas, flies, mosquitoes, blister beetles, and more. Spiders, unlike many of these other monsters, are not trying to eat you. In fact, they're almost always trying to get out of your way, and bite only when surprised, for example when you surprise one tangled up in your bedding.

A few spiders commonly found in Maine do have, on those startling occasions, the capacity to make you remember the encounter, though the severity of the experience depends partly on your sensitivity to the venom. Among species common in Maine, some wolf spiders (Lycosidae) and some jumping spiders (Saliticidae), who both hunt rather than snare, can clamp into your skin enough to give you a start. But again, they get out of your way first, and bite as a last resort.

A boogey-spider whose name evokes black-widow-like fear is the brown recluse, identified by a distinct violin shape on its back. Its venom can kill skin cells, raise a nasty, painful volcano of a wound, and in very unusual cases cause renal failure and death. Loxosceles reclusa, however, does not live in Maine, and is identified only rarely as a stowaway in luggage or shipping from south.

Years ago I had such a volcano-like bitehole that after a week or so hurt so much I went to the doctor, who speculated it was a brown recluse bite. In light of what the arachnologists say, though, if it was a spider, it was more likely a sac spider (family Clubionidae), some species of which do live in these parts, who probably got annoyed while poking around in my shirt or sheets. Their venom contains a cytotoxin that can cause a painful, necrotizing wound like the one I had, but it's not deadly. I still live.

Black widow bites, though, can be fatal. Their venom is a neurotoxin, meaning it's poisonous to nerve tissue. The bite itself is by all accounts practically unnoticeable, but the neurotoxin eventually raises a dull ache around the wound that can be followed by severe abdominal pain, muscle spasms, difficulty breathing, and in extreme cases death, though this is unusual, especially as there are antidotes. Like virtually all spiders, the black widows avoid you first, and bite last; in fact, as spiders go, they're relatively shy and retiring.

So should Jack be living in black widow fear?

Well, maybe, but really, no. Black widows, when they do appear in Maine, have traveled from points south and are not living here. For now, at least.

The pest control entomologists at the University of Maine say they see a half dozen or so black widows a year, most of which turn up in grapes traveling from much warmer climes to a grocery store in Maine. They're usually of the Western widow species (L. hesperus) or sometimes a brown widow (L. geometricus).

They're not established in Maine, entomologist Don Barry told me, at least as of the summer of 2015. If winters moderate, he said, they could start setting up their quiet cobweb shops and churning out offspring that survive to live another summer.

But for now, no worries. Running across a black widow spider in Maine is not impossible, but it's very unlikely because they don't live here and they stay out of your way.

The real annoyance is the fear.

The Ticks Don't Care

Years ago when I taught at Unity College, the outdoor recreation professors drilled a sentence into every generation of students: "The woods don't care."

It meant that along with being remarkably beautiful, the forest is remarkably dangerous. The oaks and cathedral-like firs do no more than stand there when you're lost and running out of daylight. They stand there all night, too, unmoved, and on into the next morning.

It's hard to think of a tree as a threat. It just doesn't care. But its inhabitants, like ticks, are a clue about the warning's depth. They can scare the pants off you.

They're tiny. Some are a quarter-inch wide, but a lot of them, like the deer tick, are just lumbering specks. If one finds you, it burrows into your skin and drinks your blood. It can inject bacteria into you. If you don't carefully tweezer it off your scalp or ankle, the body tears away and the maw gets stuck. The whole head stays in your skin, digging deeper. Bad infections can follow.

One of the bad infections is Lyme disease, caused by a bacteria the ticks get from biting deer and mice. It usually starts with a rash, fever, headache, and muscle or joint pain. After weeks the pain can get worse, and after months mental instabilities can set in. Tick-borne Lyme disease has become a matter of concern in the Northeast. The incidence rate in Maine soared from fewer than ten cases per one hundred thousand people in 2001 to more than a hundred per hundred thousand people in 2014, with the highest rate of infection along Maine's Midcoast.

But the ticks don't care about that, and neither do the deer who feed them, and neither does their habitat.

Years ago some friends and I went camping on Little Chebeague Island in Casco Bay. We walked around the beach from the ferry stop on Big Chebeague and at low tide crossed the sandbar to Little Chebeague, which at that time was overgrown and wild. We found a huge, gorgeous oak tree in a grassy clearing and set up our tents under it.

While my friends took a campers' nap, I got restless and walked down to a rocky beach to ruminate on the beauty of Maine and its seascapes – the wild rose thickets yellowing in the September sunlight, the glistening blue water. Signs of the divine.

Standing on the silent beach, I took off my hat and ran my fingers through my hair. (It was a long time ago.) I felt a scab. Odd. It came loose. Then I felt another one. It came loose, too.

On my neck was another one, and wondering what the hell was going on I brushed it away. I took off my shirt and saw motion in the collar and seams. Ticks. Multilegged. Crawling. Ravenous.

I shook out the shirt and looked in my hat – the inside band was teeming. I took my pants off, and in the seams and zipper were ticks, ticks, more ticks. I brushed, flapped and picked until they seemed gone, and then I stripped and dove into the cold salt water and stayed under to soak off whatever monsters remained.

I don't know, it must have worked. I got dressed and walked back to tell my friends. We had a collective vision of ticks dropping like paratroopers out of the oak tree to feast on us and leave us for dead.

The woods do not care.

Fatal Attraction

At the top of our driveway grows a white flower of unknown species. Every summer when it starts blossoming in July, I make my way down the embankment through the grass, day lilies and bedstraws, take a couple of samples and pictures, and then head back to the Shed where the wildflower books are.

Years later, I'm still not sure what the flower is. One thing I do know, though, is that I'm not going to eat it.

For a long time we called it Queen Anne's lace, whose tiny white blossoms grow in an umbel shaped like a galaxy or a flat moon – just like the unknown flower. Queen Anne's lace is also called bird's nest because it curls up at night into a little nest-like ovoid. Also wild carrot because the root is like a small carrot and can be dug up, cooked and eaten; Waldo County naturalist Tom Seymour says cultivating your Queen Anne's lace will, after some generations, result in a larger root like a garden carrot.

But the umbel of the flower by the driveway is sparser than most Queen Anne's lace, and it doesn't have the tiny purple floret in the middle, as the wild carrot often does. You'd think this would be a helpful clue to identifying it. But you'd be wrong. There are several other flowers that look so much like these two that from a distance it's hard to tell them apart.

And up close, it turns out, some of them can kill you.

Like water hemlock. To the unpracticed eye, it kind of resembles Queen Anne's lace. But when you key it out with a book, you find differences. Water hemlock has a smooth, purple-streaked stem. Its umbels are similar to those of Queen

Anne's lace but tend – tend, mind you – to be more domed than flattened. Queen Anne's lace has a bristly stem and tiny leaflets called bracts hanging under the flowers, while water hemlock does not. The invisible difference is that water hemlock contains cicutoxin, which is a powerful neurotoxin.

In October 1992, according to a Centers for Disease Control Report, two brothers, twenty-three and thirty-nine years old, were searching in the woods of Midcoast Maine for ginseng, whose blossom looks something like water hemlock. They apparently thought they might have found some because they both chewed into the root, the younger biting off more than the older.

"Within 30 minutes," the report says, "the younger man vomited and began to have convulsions; they walked out of the woods, and approximately 30 minutes after the younger man became ill, they were able to telephone for emergency rescue services.

"Within 15 minutes of the call, emergency medical personnel arrived and found the younger man unresponsive and cyanotic with mild tachycardia, dilated pupils, and profuse salivation. Severe tonic-clonic seizures occurred and were followed by periods of apnea. He was intubated and transported to a local emergency department. Physicians performed gastric lavage and administered activated charcoal. His cardiac rhythm changed to ventricular fibrillation, and four resuscitative attempts were unsuccessful. He died approximately three hours after ingesting the root."

The older brother developed seizures and delirium within a couple of hours, but he lived.

The root they ate was from water hemlock (Cicuta maculata, aka spotted cowbane), which killed five people in the United States between 1979 and 1988.

The thing is, there are a number of other plants that they could have mistaken for ginseng, dangerous or not.

Ginseng looks less like water hemlock than do water parsnip, cow parsnip (aka hogweed), Scotch lovage, hemlock parsley and caraway, all of which grow around here, have edible parts, and look very much alike – which is to say not only like water hemlock, but also like bulb-bearing water hemlock and poison hemlock, both of which can also be fatal to ingest.

In a range of resemblance to water hemlock or ginseng are yarrow, whose feathery-looking little leaves are quick studies, and valerian, whose root can be turned into a sedative tea. I was attracted into a field by some lovely umbels that turned out to belong, not to valerian, but to a nice, healthy water hemlock. When I got up close I was pretty sure what it was but wanted to key it out in a book, so I broke it off at the ground where a few drops of sap fell out. Later I learned the cicutoxin can be absorbed through your skin.

The flower at the top of the driveway has a grooved stem and is not mottled purple, so I'm pretty sure it isn't water hemlock. It has characteristics of hemlock parsley, caraway and Queen Anne's lace, but not all of any of them.

I'm sure someone can tell what it is, but it isn't me, and I'm not going to test it by chewing the root.

Out of the Howling Darkness

One summer night a tremendous commotion split the darkness in the driveway. There was a chaotic scrabbling sound, then one of the cats screamed. The younger one, we thought from the voice.

As we made our way to the window to look out, a high-pitched, retching barking sounded, in rhythmic yelps. The cat hissed and spit.

We turned the outside lights on. A fox was pacing back and forth in front of the garage. The cat was trapped in there under the car. Her eyes glowed under the bumper.

The fox was not immediately fazed by the lights. The choking barks continued and the fox maneuvered near the garage doorway, trying to terrify the cat into dashing for the woods.

I stepped quietly to the other car parked by the front door, and turned on the headlights. They flooded the driveway and front of the garage with a ghostly, artificial glow. The fox got confused and darted up the driveway, then down, then back again, not wanting to let the cat-meal go. The cat, presumably understanding what the sudden radiance meant and keeping her wits, continued to crouch under the car.

Finally the fox ran for the trees, the cacophony ended, and the summer evening quietly reassembled. An hour or two later, the cat scratched at the door as usual.

Weird sounds come out of the woods at night. Some nights the coyotes howl. It's sort of a high-pitched baritone, and it has a definite beauty that's encased in lurking wildness – the terror of whatever's out there. Sometimes there's crashing, stamping and heavy snorting near the back door, too close for comfort. I awoke in the dark once to hear a frighteningly loud slavering-growling straight out of a living-dead horror movie right outside the bedroom window. I peered out, afraid I would see one of the cats being torn to pieces by – what? It was too dark to see any more than a large doglike shape near the lilac bush. But the sound of grisly slobbering rending was horrific.

When the cows at the dairy farm miles away bawl during the day it's like a kind of cute yodeling, but at night you wonder if it's a choir of the damned. The birds all hush at night – except for the occasional owl doing exactly what owls, like foxes, are supposed to do – but then sing again at sunrise.

Our optimism tells us the first created thing was light. "Let there be light," the God of Moses, Jesus and Muhammad says. But before the light came on, there had to be the sound of that voice. The Sufis say all music is an echo of that first note that brought order to the chaos. Out of the howling darkness comes bird song.

Exercising Your Moral Compartments

One late-July day, there was a dead body under the deck.

I couldn't tell what it was at first because its head was mangled and twisted around backward. The body was bent at angles not usually seen in three-dimensional space. Rodent-like eyes were glaring in two or three different directions, lights out. Flies were feasting on dried blood under the remains of the face. The fur had been raked, but seemed too brown and smooth to belong to what in happier times might have been a squirrel.

Well aware the flies would multiply and a mucky stench would ensue as natural processes took over the disanimated flesh, I retrieved from the garage a shovel and noticed, when the carcass flopped aboard, that the departed had been a rabbit. When it was alive, it was probably cute.

I knew who the slaying suspects were. At that moment they were sleeping lazily among the tomato-plant pots a few feet away. Hard to piece together, from a certain frame of reference, that the same two who were purring with pleasant contentment also twisted and tore to pieces this little rabbit, who was for all intents and purposes himself harmless. Harmless to us, I mean.

As I trudged to the woods holding the shovel level like a bier, I undertook a thought experiment to imagine what the rabbit experienced. It's well along the way to being admitted by a preponderance of scientists that animals experience emotions that are at least parallel, if not similar or even identical to ours. So it's probably accurate to imagine that this rabbit probably died terrified. I'll spare you the rest of the nightmarish guesswork.

The cats participate in two apparently separate worlds: ours and, one step smaller, the woods of rabbits, squirrels, chipmunks, blue jays, voles and field mice. In our world they seem to be guided by certain moral behaviors such as friendship, loyalty, discretion in cleanliness, and if you can believe it, justice. (Try giving one cat food and affection, but not the other, and see what happens.) In the woods world, they're cold-blooded killers. And so are the fishers that, at roughly the same bio-level of forest fauna, attack and dismember cats.

The birds share that same bio-space with the cats, and sometimes pay the same price the cats pay fishers and foxes. Birds engage in various moral (or at least, moral-looking) behaviors such as child-rearing, nesting duties and territory watching. They share space with the next bio-level down the way we share space with cats – birds practice on insects and spiders the same terrors that cats practice on rabbits and fishers practice on cats.

Whether a spider can be "terrified" is of course an empirically unanswerable question, although studies of spider fear have concluded, for instance, that some individuals of the same species are braver than others. Courage being, as we recall, one of the basic moral virtues valued in essentially all human cultures.

We're so much bigger than our local spiders that normally we hardly notice them, even though most of the time there's at least one within three feet of you. When we do notice them, as often as not the reaction is to squash it and forget it. Same with beetles, ants, etc. Things that small are out of our moral range.

Birds and rabbits are big enough to warrant a different kind of attention, in at least two ways. One is they have human-like qualities of physiognomy and behavior that attract us emotionally. The other is that we eat them. The way cats, for example, eat rabbits.

When the cat tears the rabbit limb from limb, a certain feeling of moral proximity to the rabbit might spur indignation or even rage toward the cat. But as far as anyone can tell, those moral feelings are completely outside the cat's understanding. When we eat a nice chicken salad, though, the same exact range of blood-curdling terror once electrified the sauteed chunks of meat. It's just been artificially disappeared by the transcendent human ability to mentally compartmentalize everything. But you know, we kill and eat birds, rabbits, deer and cows (of all things) the same way birds eat spiders and spiders eat flies.

The corpse under the deck was kind of a shock. That shock results from us humans inhabiting a moral consciousness larger and more complex than that of a cat. But the moral overlap from human to cat, to bird and rabbit, to spider is quite a bit larger than you normally think. A spider tooling innocently along the kitchen counter only to be suddenly annihilated by a whack from some unseen upper world experiences a cosmos similar to ours, where what seem for all the world like unseen forces sometimes converge to suddenly obliterate us on a highway, or on a golf course in a lightning storm, or in the driveway shoveling snow.

If ants had nuclear weapons, E.O. Wilson once said, they'd destroy the world in two weeks.

Who are we? Where are we? And what are those lazy cats doing now?

Cat Karma

One Sunday morning we went outside to the deck for our coffee and found a familiar sight: The two cats, Brian and Panda, were sleeping under the chairs in the warm, bugless, clear air. A little earlier they had eaten their complimentary canned-food breakfast. The bear-cub-like orange one, Brian, who shows all the signs of Maine coon cat ancestry, was stretched flat on his side, eyes asquint, claws kneading slowly in and out, purring.

"These cats must have done some really good deeds in their past lives to be living like this now," I said.

"Brian probably did," Bonnie said as she settled into her sunny chair with her cup, "but not Panda."

Brian, who then was five years old, had the reputation of being cool, calm, collected and kind (except to small creatures like the unfortunate vole whose body was offered before sunrise to square with Bonnie's feet). Panda, who was about three, was the household equivalent of the village idiot. He was so completely untroubled there among the pots of plants with his dream-scampering feet that his fur might as well have been black and white pajamas.

"You mean Panda's cashing in good karma he hasn't earned yet?" I said.

"No, it's not that," she replied. "Brian appreciates what he's got. You can tell. When he lounges around like this and rubs against your leg and comes to greet you when you drive up in the car, he's spreading around gratitude. When Panda does it, he just wants the pats."

"But Panda's not mean," I said. "He's just a fool."

"That's exactly what I'm saying. Panda doesn't know how good he's got it. He just expects it. He thinks this is just the way it is."

"But Panda seems so happy to see you when you drive up. He rolls around in the dirt just like Brian."

"But Brian understands he's being provided for, and Panda doesn't. Brian's an older soul," she said.

Now part of what she meant was that Brian had a life-changing experience when he was about a year old. He was stalking in the trees partway down the driveway when Jack drove up with one of his buddies. They must have startled Brian, and he leapt straight into the car's grill. They ran to get me, and when I saw him lying there, I thought he was dead. We took him to the vet even though he seemed beyond salvation. Long story short, after an overnight stay he came back to life, but with a headache that appeared to last for months. We think that old catastrophe still encroaches on him in the form of recurring headaches and being excessively jumpy at sudden noises. But he also turned into a very affectionate and knowingly intelligent, and seemingly – if anthropomorphization is allowed – appreciative cat.

Panda on the other hand has never seemed to understand how good he's got it, or anything else for that matter. Jack rescued him from a cardboard box under a counter in a scroungy pet shop. He was red-eyed, dirty, bone-skinny and bug-infested. He had terrors for days after he arrived at our house, and Brian was none too happy about his presence. But eventually he settled into the routine of breakfast, sleeping, prowling abundant woods, and also witlessly doing every possible ridiculous thing a cat can do – scratching almost without fail to come inside just about twelve to thirty seconds after you've settled into a chair in the living room; repeatedly failing to make corners and crashing into walls; slipping one body part at a time off the deck railing and finally splattering on the ground; sleeping in the middle of the driveway forgetting that cars do not go around him. Once I was sitting with a very sore, freshly bandaged toe in the living room when Panda wandered over and stepped directly on it, placing all his weight on one paw and the toe.

In other words, Panda does not seem to have learned anything. Brian, on the other hand, seems to have deep-seated cat wisdom. He knows by innate cat intuition not to step on my injured toe. What this implies, in Bonnie's cosmology, is gratitude on Brian's part and complacent greed on Panda's part.

"Panda's operating on karmic credit and is going to have to pay for it, is what it seems like to me," I said.

"It's not that simple," Bonnie said. "You can't make a balance sheet of karma. It's not like a checkbook with one-to-one expenses and credits. It's a whole complication of factors that interplay among themselves over long periods of time."

"Over cat lifetimes?" I said.

She shrugged. "Who knows. What you do comes back to you, my grandmother used to say."

She sipped her coffee and cut up an orange. A green-glinting hummingbird buzzed our heads, and a squad of mourning doves suddenly scattered on beating wings into the firs and cedars. The cats looked up, then went back to their rest.

Mañana, mañana.

The Troy Declaration on Consciousness

It's a few minutes after noon. Brian is curled up on the bed.

"Brian. You slept on the chair all night," I say. "Now you're going to sleep on the bed all day?"

He opens one eye, purrs three or four strokes as if to say, "It's cool, brother," and settles back into some parallel cat dimension.

I wonder what he's doing while he's asleep. It seems obvious he dreams, because he twitches and whimpers. In humans these are signs of a REM state. Whatever it is, Brian spends huge swaths of time there.

Of course, he's only a cat. (His tufted ears, burly shoulders, thick orange hair and massive, dangerous claws suggest he's probably got Maine coon cat genes, but no one knows for sure. He might just be huge.) "Only a cat," I say, though Brian is an intellectual, if lackadaisical, genius in comparison to his black and white sidekick, Panda.

From one point of view this catthropomorphizing is an amusing but kind of meaningless sort of hyperbole because for a long time, science has denied that animals have anything like rational intelligence. There is just no way to know, empirically, whether animals think. So it has been assumed they act on instinct, and humans are the only people with conscious intelligence.

Of course, anyone who has ever lived with dogs or cats knows how naïve this assumption is. Dogs and cats have definite individual personalities, and some are smarter than others.

Poe describes a cat of his that carried out a complicated process of opening a latched door.

And twenty-four hundred years ago Socrates observed that dogs are philosophers. Think about it, he says in *The Republic*. A dog distinguishes friends or family members from strangers. When a friend approaches, he welcomes him. When a stranger comes in the yard, he gets angry (or, in the case of a trusting dog like a Labrador, he investigates). This means the dog bases his actions on knowledge. Which is what philosophers do. A dog is a philosopher.

So is a cat, though of a more existential ilk. Cats base their actions on a refined knowledge of routines. Brian scrambles off the chair when he hears the top pop on a can of cat food. He heads for the woods when the younger grandchildren start piling out of cars. He comes out to greet us when he hears our cars, and hides in the garage when unfamiliar vehicles pull in.

Cats' knowledge of routines can actually be too refined. A veterinarian once told me that in an experiment, some cats were taught (pretty quickly, I imagine) to follow a daily path to a food dish. When the path was blocked off for a few days, the cats nearly starved because, while they smartly knew the routine, they could not outthink it. Panda could easily starve with food right around the corner. I have a feeling Brian would find the dish because for him, food trumps everything.

To me the phrase "dumb animals" is meaningless. Crows are fully cognizant of where vehicles do and do not drive: They go about their business undisturbed in the breakdown lane, but scatter from the travel lanes – they seem to understand the painted lines. Dragonflies and jumping spiders watch what you're doing, possibly calculating whether you pose any danger. Cuttlefish, cousins of the octopus, learn to find their way around mazes. Bees, it is reported, can recognize a particular human face in photographs.

Even the scientists have acknowledged that animals are more than electrically animated meat Popsicles.

"The Cambridge Declaration on Consciousness," drawn up by a conference of neuroscientists and neurophysiologists in July 2012, states: "The weight of evidence indicates that humans are not unique in possessing the neurological substrates that generate consciousness. Nonhuman animals, including all mammals and birds, and many other creatures, including octopuses, also possess these neurological substrates."

Dog and cat owners have known this for a long time, by other means than statistical studies of brain activity.

At night when it's time to go either downstairs or outside, neither Brian nor Panda wants to go because they both know (see above: Socrates' dog) that it's dark downstairs, possibly cold outside, and more comfortable shedding hair on the living room furniture.

Panda, possessing more substrate than neurology, lacks the imagination to make any waves except on impulse, and usually just submits to the routine. Brian has some kind of cat thermostat that knows the outdoor temperature, and volunteers to go out when it's above 45, but filters toward the basement door when it's below 45. Filters reluctantly.

He gets this sour look on his face, with sort of squinty eyes and ears twitching back but not flattening like with full-on anger. Just very irritated. Sometimes he pauses in case somebody changes their mind at the last minute.

One night Bonnie nudged him out of this pause with her foot. He squinted into the distance. But knowing the routine, he stepped down.

"He'd give us the finger if he could," Bonnie said, closing the door. "He wouldn't turn around. Just over his shoulder, while he walks away."

Blue Angels

On August 9, the purple martins were swooping and darting over the Unity baseball fields and popping in and out of their pole-top condominium just as they had since the flock arrived in May. On August 11, all was eerily quiet. They had vanished into thin air.

The southward migration of the martins, it turns out, begins in mid-August. They arrive in Maine during April or May, usually preceded by a few "scouts" who are older birds that know the landscape and come ahead of the rest to check on last summer's digs, which they strongly prefer. If everything is copacetic the later-arriving families move in and set to work feathering nests and laying four or five white eggs. Copacetic – or to use the less casual technical phrase "site fidelity" – means the place is still clean, solid, handy to water and unobstructed by trees or other skyscrapers so they can swoop and swerve in and out of the roost. It helps if there's no immediate threat from starlings or house sparrows, who will knock eggs out of the nest to crack them open and sometimes actually kill adult martins.

Purple martins (Progne subis) are the largest dominion of swallows that frequent our sky. Their relatives are barn swallows (with rusty orange bellies), cliff swallows and tree swallows. They're exceptionally gregarious, and how many martins will fit in a birdhouse – or on the head of a pin – depends mainly on the size of your imagination of a residence. Audubon says they'll dwell in anything from a one-room efficiency to a two-hundred-unit complex. They travel together in even larger flocks to their winter homes as far as deepmost South America, though it is apparently not known exactly which flocks fly how far south.

People have been cheered by purple martins since literally time immemorial. The early European settlers noticed that the Indians put gourds on tall poles around their gardens for the martins to nest in, and imitated the tactic by constructing bird houses because the martins are bug-eaters, clearing the air of all kinds of flying demons, from midges to flies to wasps.

They do this with Blue Angel deftness. They turn, twist, dive and climb in extraordinary improvised dances on the very air. They buzz down like fighter planes if you get too close to the digs. They chatter together with tremendous energy on wing and roost, and when the sunlight strikes their dark-blue feathers, their heads burn with a blue iridescence. Their point-tipped wings in flight look like the gear of aerial spirits, and on a perch fold into upthrust shoulders like ancient depictions of angels. Which came first, the angels or the martins, I'm not sure.

The Solitary Martin

By later in August, the purple martins are a couple of weeks gone. Their southern principalities, no doubt, are by that time beginning to fill with the same perennial here-and-goneness of their cycle.

One year, a day or two after the early August vamoose from the bird condominiums at the Unity park, I stopped in to make the walking-path circuit, got out of the car, and saw sitting on the chain link fence near the baseball field fifty or sixty feet west of the condo, a solitary martin. The martins are normally chattery-loud, but this one, with a kind of scruffy, old-man look, struck only a single little chirp in irregular time. The air was otherwise quiet in the flock's conspicuous absence. Fat seconds, a minute, two or three would go by silent, then he'd chirp again in that tenor-sounding purple martin voice.

What was he doing by himself, quiet and mostly unmoving except for the occasional hunch of a shoulder or twitch of the head?

I listened, motionless myself, for ten minutes or so, then strolled the kilometer-round of the park. When I got back he was still there, singing one plaintive note every timeless little while. My mind wandered onto the notion that he was posted there to round up the stragglers who missed the general southward out-winging a day or two before. This modulated the whole afternoon, the hazy clouds, the woods, the declining summer lake light deep into a minor key. The martin alone on the fence chipped an inexpressible autumn melancholy right into the spot of time itself.

In about half an hour, two other martins materialized over the baseball field. In the outfield, crows meanwhile were parading around and scolding each other. A couple of gulls didn't know whether to fly or just keep complaining. The two martins darted in and out of the birdhouse, chattering cheerily, tardy though they were in my ornithocosmic scheme. After a few minutes of their aerial nonsense, the solitary martin stretched out his wings and took off, made a few loops around the grounds, a few airborne chips of sound, and then dematerialized in the haze.

It just seemed unutterably sad. The last purple martin posted like an avian elder to round up the last of the flock. The first sign of fall. The loneliness, loss or natural sorrow that is the inner shape of the sadness – so Poe said – that is connected with certain revelations of beauty. Or whatever you call that piercing feeling you get when September strikes.

Unsure of anything but the feeling itself, I asked one of my birding advisers if this geriatric-seeming bird was indeed a sort of end-of-summer counterpart to the scouts who arrive early in spring to check out last year's digs before the rest arrive.

First of all, she said, the bird was not old, but probably in some stage of molt, possibly even young. And second, birds don't guide each other through migration. Why one sat by itself on the fence for an hour, we'll never be able to say.

The next day, as it happened, the birdhouse was a clattering chaos of martins again. They had not left after all. Unless this was a whole different flock passing through. No way to know that, either.

So in ornithological fact, my whole hour brooding over the solitary martin was a complete fantasy. The lonely late-summer sense of an approaching ending toward inevitable fall and winter and all its natural metaphors was, for all intents and purposes, a self-made mirage.

This put me in mind of another recurrently spoken-of incident from decades ago. A friend and I were visiting the home in Waldoboro of an eminent poet, when we stepped outside to look at a particularly rosy winter sunset. Studying one unusual-looking streak in the sky, I said, "I think that might be the comet" (which was reportedly visible in the sky at the time). This got my two friends excited and we talked about comets and other seemingly related aesthetic experiences long into the evening.

Uneasy about the facts of reality, as usual, I later went to the library (no Googling in those days) to find out exactly where the comet was, and realized I was completely wrong. It must have been a jet contrail. So I wrote to the wise old poet to set him straight about what we actually saw.

He wouldn't have it. He insisted it was the comet. And he would not let it go. When I visited him in Buffalo a year or two later, and in correspondence afterward, he'd bring it up and flatly declare that our original reading of the sky was correct: It was in fact the comet, he said again and again. Even though, I kept thinking, it was not the comet.

I don't want to get on the wrong side of the scientists.

However, there is a contentious issue in philosophy sometimes called The Mary Problem. Mary is a hypothetical neuroscientist who studies the perception and processing of light in the brain. She knows all there is to know about how photons enter the eye, strike the retina, process through rod and cone cells down through optic nerves and deep into the places where your biochemicals register shapes, colors and motion. She knows all there is to know about the physical properties and behaviors of light and sight.

One minor detail: Mary has lived her whole life only in a room with no color, only black, white and gray light. So when she steps out of the room for the first time and perceives blue, suddenly she knows something about light that she didn't know when she knew everything about it.

There is more to reality, this argument concludes, than the physical facts. The framer of The Mary Problem also adds the non-hypothetical fact that while we know there is an ultraviolet color, we don't know what it looks like because we can't see it. Some insects, spiders and birds, however, *can* see it, so in this epistemological scheme, they know things we don't.

What does all this have to do with the solitary martin. Nothing you can say solves it. Despite my completely mistaken ornithological speculations about his presence on the fence at the Unity park, the autumn loneliness of that moment is with me like a gorgeous melody long after, as real as a cascading blue autumn sky.

A Few More Words about Goldenrod

Every summer, the goldenrod transpiring in the fields and roadsides spellbinds my eye, and this leads inevitably to wanting to talk about them. To try to reproduce, or mirror, or evoke them in words as accurately as possible. Every summer I find myself trying again. And finding every summer that the words are never exactly accurate to the golden facts, I start to feel like Giacometti, who tried again and again to make a nose out of clay that seemed accurate to the spirit of the human form but, in his eyes at least, never quite succeeded. He just kept trying.

So it is with me for the goldenrods. Please forgive the repetition. They materialize in July like apparitions in fields and along roadsides. Spraying clusters of tiny bright-yellow flowers, some bent gently over as if weighed down by a breeze, others in cubist sky-pointing arrowheads, and still others flat, almost like their cousin the tansy.

Goldenrod is diverse upon diverse. In the family Asteracea (a weirdly accurate word built from the ancient Greek for star) and the genus Solidago (from a Latin root meaning roughly to make whole or solid), there are one hundred twenty-five or more species in North America. How many occur in Maine I don't know, but it's more than you can name confidently working only part-time.

Their blossoms express five general forms, according to one field guide: plumelike, elm-branched, clublike, wandlike and flat-topped. Most common in my parlance are the rough-stemmed, Canada and lance-leaved goldenrods. Also in our range are sweet, tall, early, late and slender-fragrant goldenrods; stout, showy, downy, gray and hairy; large-leaved, rough-leaved, elm-leaved, blue-stemmed and zigzag; Alpine (on mountains), silverrod, northern bog and seaside; Rand's and Elliott's.

No doubt there are more – they have the unusual capacity to cross-breed, some with each other and some even with other Asteraceas. The root of the Canada goldenrod, according to one book, was used by Indians for burns, and the flowers were chewed to ease sore throat; the leaves can be used to make a diuretic, anti-inflammatory tea. The leaves of sweet goldenrod have a scent like anise and make a tea pleasant to the tongue.

Goldenrod energies take form in flowers that feel simultaneously heavy and light, as though they were tough – which they clearly are, as they root practically anywhere sunlight pours down freely and no one hays or mows – but also ethereal, suspended on the air at the tops of their stalks in astounding pyramids, floes and angularities that seem to be emerging from other dimensions entirely.

They fascinate me more than any sculpture. Every summer they stream together in fields or grow alone as if wandering toward a new group. Year in and year out they unceasingly form and re-form living, breathing vitalities of unbelievable complexity and slant. So every summer up pop these verbal weeds, trying to reproduce this perennial facet of summer.

The World in a Grain of Scent

Late August. Deep in the most beautiful three or four months of the New England year.

The air is turning crisp at night, the Sun is finding its autumn angles, the purple martins are gone. Red leaves are already fringing Carlton Bog.

And in one of those glittering everyday invisibilities, like the dinosaur fossils that were everywhere for eons but hardly noticed until the eighteenth century, the scent of late summer is visiting down through the pines and settling into September.

Late summer, I mean, smells different from mudfetid March and even loamy May. For one thing the grass odor is dry. Out of it breathes that strong sweet-cut scent, with sometimes surrounding it the bite of wild carrot – Queen Anne's lace – when it gets mowed. On hot afternoons are tingling pitch and pine incenses, and the carpets of needles like a dry spice of the north woods. All now.

These odors have, to me, always blurred into one late-summer smell that I've hardly paid attention to, like a zodiacal glow in the peripheral vision of the nose. The way all colors blend together in white, late-summer smells seem to blend together, too.

A study recently showed that humans – though our olfactory capabilities are ten thousand to one hundred thousand times weaker than dogs' – can distinguish about a trillion different odors. It's hard for the scientists to tell exactly because there's no continuum of scent, the way there's a continuum of colors on the spectrum. Maybe this is because light travels in waves of energy while odors come on molecules, physically diving and darting on the breeze rather than refracting through atmosphere. Some insects are thought to zigzag so much because it's the most efficient way to pick up the odor-molecules dancing from flowers where the nectar is and, by the way, the pollen grains.

There may be no spectrum of smells, but there is this unity of many scents. The pile of cut, split wood dumped last week in front of the garage radiates that redolence of sap and pulp. If you pay attention your nose can sort the dry-grass smell underneath it. And something else, which turns out to be the toadflax, or butter-and-eggs flowers, which up close smell so strong and sweet it's practically perfume.

The miniature grove of euphrasia next to the woodpile is too faintly scented to detect directly, but with your face down next to them you realize they're blending into the woodscent too. Them, and the St. Johnswort, faintsweet, the hawkweed blossoms with a distant microbouquet, and the Canada thistle, stronger. Dirt-sour crabapples are already hitting the ground. At night, a skunk. By the driveway I found a late wild-madder patch wispily pungent in the grass, and burdock, a sort of floralwood to my inefficient nose. If you strip a twig from a yellow birch, you get the bite of wintergreen.

Some goldenrods my nose is too dull to detect, but some, like the lance-leaved goldenrod, are honeylike. There's a grasslike tang to most of their leaves, and sweet-goldenrod leaves, when crushed, smell like anise.

Along the embankment at the top of the driveway, a grove of white flowers grows that we used to assume was all Queen Anne's lace. Tiny white flowers in compound umbels shaped like galaxies. But while wild carrot is among them – identifiable by a purple floret and bracts under the umbels – most of these are not Queen Anne's lace. What they are, I don't know. These are the flowers that summer after summer I key out with books but can't identify. They're not valerian or ginseng. Not water hemlock, poison hemlock, Scotch lovage, or any parsnip known to Maine. They most resemble caraway or hemlock parsley, but they're not.

What they are is fragrant beyond belief. Collectively they radiate a rich, fruitlike fullness that floats down the breeze long before you see them. It overflows the air among the tall grass, goldenrod and white sweet clover up there. These unnameable wildflowers are an essence of the Pure Lands escaping into Maine, I'm convinced of it. The universe is filled with their light.

When this scent is pervading the top of the driveway, the season of mists and mellow fruitfulness is about to congeal out of late summer. Soon the woods will be stacking fallen leaves. Acorns will tumble like rain onto the Shed roof, roll down and split on the ground. The full-on scent of autumn, October oak and cool air is due. Eternity in an olfactory hour.

The Urge for Staying

Late summer is always a surprise, even though you can see it coming by mid-July.

Patches of meadow grass redden and brown. Goldenrod sends up the first ranks of its empire. Dusty-pink steeplebush blossoms poke from bushes, and purple loosestrife and Queen Anne's lace come up in droves. Fireweed. Except for a few days of rain and the odd thunderstorm, the air keeps a sultry, summer-colored haze into August. Then, about the time the dragonflies have cleared the yard of bugs and Bonnie has unpacked her grade books to get ready for school, it strikes all at once, like the wallop of God.

Suddenly the air is fantastically clear and cool. The green of the woods blackens, as if night was unfolding in the trees and bringing every needle into relief. The distance over the hills from Dixmont to the western mountains looks measurable not just in miles, but in age. This place is ancient. You can see through the undershadow almost into the past. Who prowled these woods, and where, and for how long, before Europeans came and cut the pines?

The corn has peaked, but it's not that, and it's not that the apples are soon to be ripe. But it's the air itself, the northwest wind sweeping out the Shed and drying firewood, as if a great door opened and pitch and juniper scents have saturated the atmosphere. This whole corner of creation feels clean.

It starts earlier some years than others. In one mid-August trip to Quebec I saw fields of wall-to-wall goldenrod and clots of orange and red leaves huddled in maples near Jackman. But those were signs of fall – premature, and not what I'm talking about.

At the moment of late summer, winter is not yet closing in. Frost has not yet perched in the garden, and the geese do not yet have the urge to fly off in the majestic chevrons that ripple your blood. The wind is cool but doesn't bite. The Sun is not yet traitor-cold; it angles in just below July-height and heats the air. There's no temptation yet to lock yourself in and wait for spring.

Instead, this is what April promised all along. What's here is now fully alive. The air magnifies the black-green mountains one range beyond another. Sunlight grapples with shadow patches on steel-blue lakes. Hay rolls diminish into the distance in fields. Everything is deep. It's exactly what maturity looks like before decline.

The Earth's most transcendently beautiful conditions of atmosphere, sunlight and shadow are revealed here in late August. It's as if a living being had descended, for just a month or so, and put the final polish on everything. You could stay in Maine forever.

Chebeague Island and the Tides of Time

What thou lovest well remains,

the rest is dross

– Ezra Pound, Canto LXXXI

In the blue distance of inner Casco Bay, the smokestacks of the Cousins Island power plant poked into the sky. 1980, this was, looking northeast from an alcove window of a third-floor apartment on the Eastern Promenade in Portland, where I lived that summer.

East of the smokestacks across the water was a strand of white beach. This marked Little Chebeague Island, which I had cruised past in many boats and flown over in seaplanes many times, but where I had never set foot. Farther on were the green-black shadows of Great Chebeague, where I had set many feet. It looked uncapturably, wistfully far away. More like an echo off the water than a real place.

"Wistful" barely describes my state of mind when I looked through those windows. It was more like the ache you feel when you can't get the lyrics to bubble out of a melody echoing in your head – *what song is that?* – only further in. Would I ever live in my childhood home again?

The Eastern Abenaki word transliterated as "Chebeague" means, according to various sources, either "wide expanse of water," or "island of many springs," or "separated place." Any of these will do, but the last seems closest because the root is "sebe," meaning divided or almost-through, with the suffix "-ague," meaning beneath: Great Chebeague and Little

Chebeague are connected by a sandbar at low tide that goes beneath the water at high tide, separating the two islands.

In the mid-1950s my father, mother, little sister Heidi and I lived there. My father commuted by boat from Chandler's Cove wharf to his construction job on the power plant being newly raised on Cousins Island. He ran a flat-bottomed punt with an outboard motor to work, I knew – or at least, remember knowing.

Sometimes I rode in the bow as that punt zipped along bang-banging on minor chop between Indian Point and Little Chebeague. Looking down into the clear water at the sand rushing along beneath, the spray, and the smell of salt water, and thinking: *Is it too late to beat the tide? Will we run aground?*

One day we made the trip to Cousins Island and then to Portland, where I got an orange plastic boat in a department store, maybe W.T. Grant's. When we got back to the house we lived in somewhere on the east side of the island, I realized I had left the little boat in a brown paper bag on the ledges at Cousins Island. I knew exactly where it was, lying there in the bag. Maybe I could still find it now, sixty years later if it was still there. But it's not.

There was no going back for it that evening. Maybe that was the first of ten thousand sleepless nights. But sometime afterward, maybe the next day, maybe several days, we journeyed back over the sandbar and tied up at the landing at Cousins Island. I scrambled along the ledges, and to my astonishment and relief, the bag was exactly where I left it.

To me, even though I could not have been more than four years old, it seemed like a miracle that the boat, tucked into the bag just the way I left it, wasn't stolen or swept out to sea by waves. Where does pessimism like that come from in such a small boy, anyway?

No idea. I loved to look down into the clear green water under the pilings of the Chandler's Cove wharf at the scuttling horseshoe crabs. Ancient beyond comprehension, was the feeling, though there was no word or referable time "ancient" then. At the end of the wharf was the ramp where the ferries threw the gangplanks at low tide and passengers and freight trundled up off the boat, then down to the boat.

Whenever I could, I laid full length at the downhill end of the ramp so my eyes peered over the lip and into the water. It seemed precarious. At high tide the green water was too deep to see bottom. But I stared into it with some kind of fascination for the invisible underneath, and that feeling of teetering on the edge of safety over the literal depths turned into a dream that recurred well into my adolescence, of sliding forward and falling head first, sometimes right into the deep water, sometimes waking up afraid mid-fall, and sometimes continuing on down into the fathoms and being shocked I could still breathe, was not drowning, this is not right, but what a relief.

When the ferries arrived I got shooed back up onto the heavy, level planking on the dock, and if anybody was paying attention, well before that.

The first substantial memory of my life is of scrambling around the rocks and ledges just off the beach side of the Chandler's Cove wharf. Barnacles, seaweed and dark gray craggy rock, and across the water, what must have been a hundred or two hundred feet, boats on moorings, and on one of them was a whole float where my father tied his seaplane. Farther along the shore was the sandy beach of dry seaweed clumps and scathing, wonderful sunburns. Tied to the float attached to the wharf, punts and dinghies clattered or shifted silently in eddies like horseshoe crabs. Lobster boats quiet in the cove.

* * *

The name "Smitty" was often spoken at that time in connection with boats, and I suppose my father, along with others, had a deal with Jasper Smith to ferry them to Cousins Island when the weather or the tide was wrong to get to work at the power plant. The Chebeague Transportation Company's website history tells me, up here in the year 2015, that Smitty "began operating his water taxi between Cousins and Chebeague Island in 1959 using the Polly-Lin, a converted 36-foot lobster boat." The phrase Polly-Lin is a mythological fragment. But the location in time – I'm uneasy.

A family photo shows Heidi, who was born in 1955, at the age of about six months and me, two and a half, sitting in a field on the island. This was the day autumn was created in me. We scrambled around in the acorn-smelling woods nearby. The grass was straw brown, the air was still and chilly, the sun bright in the blue, blue sky. That day resonates like cosmic background radiation in my mind in October.

We had moved to Chebeague Island from Massachusetts, my father's native base and the place Heidi and I were born, to my mother's native Portland. My father's vocation of the moment was flying the seaplane, and I think we got to the island through arrangements by my mother's sister, who summered there, for my father to work for some sardine seiners. They hired him to spot the herring that gathered in oval schools on summer evenings.

From a few hundred feet aloft he'd search the coves of Casco Bay, then report back to the boats, angling the Piper Cub with its insect-like "floats" onto shale-flat twilight water and taxiing to where the fishermen were anchored. If fish were in one of his seiners' dory-marked coves, they'd steam out, spend the night setting and hauling nets, and cut my father in for ten percent of the take.

Sometimes I rode in the plane, and sometimes I waited on the boat. A couple of nights, probably after 1957, the year we moved off the island, my father got impressed to haul nets. I watched with anxious fascination that ancient process of pulling seines hand over hand into listing, but never capsizing dories until the fish were corralled in a space so tight that a huge hose could then be plunged directly into the school and suck them in a living, flipping, slithering, heads over tails chaotic stream into the hold of the boat. In the process, scales went everywhere, small, moon-glinting, slippery omni-everywhere on your boots and pants and down your shirt, fish scales. The smell of live fish, sharper and saltier than the smell of iced, dead market fish.

For my father this was, however, only summer work.

Construction on the William F. Wyman Station Unit 1 began in October of 1955, according to the Maine Historical Society's archival collection. That first phase of the power plant came on line in 1957 – which was the year we returned to Portland and my twin brothers, Rex and Jeff, were born.

The problem of crossing the expanse of water to Cousins Island must date from 1955 or 1956. Maybe Smitty ran the Polly-Lin as a ferry earlier than anyone but me remembers. In memory there is the diesel hum of his boat, and a certain hominess under the roofing against spray and wind and night.

There were a lot of boats. The Nellie G ferry, warm and cozy, chugging to Chandler's Wharf. The Emita, rattling and vibrating. The seining boats with rolling decks and warm galleys with coffee (not for kids). Punts and dories, outboards and rowboats, and one frightening afternoon in a gale aboard my aunt's sailboat. I wonder what part of the bay we were on when, sitting on the upper rail of the steeply heeling vessel, I feared we were capsizing, even though no one else did.

Mythic to me was the Sirius, a lobster boat by design, but larger, cleaner-lined, and equipped for seining. It belonged to Sanford Doughty, one of the fishermen my father flew for. The Sirius had a supernaturally dignified presence on its mooring in Chandler's Cove, and so did Sanford. His tall frame in oilskins and turned-down rubber boots carrying gear up the Bennetts Cove beach to his house. His laconic goodwill toward me, and his wife Mabel's too, something I hardly ever registered among adults. He took root in my mind as the prototype of wisdom and strength.

By the early '60s the herring were declining. I remember agitated discussions about purse seiners. One by one the sardine fishermen cut my father's services loose – the catches became so scant and far between they could no longer spare the ten percent to gain the edge.

My father turned the seaplane into a tourist ride. We spent several summers flying from a reed-choked berth at Great Pond in Cape Elizabeth to Mackerel Cove at Bailey Island. On autumn weekends through the mid-1960s, we spent a day on each island wharf – Long Island, Cliff, Cousins, Chebeague at Chandler's and the Stone Wharf – giving cut-rate rides to whoever had overstayed Labor Day.

While my father flew, I malingered on the docks like a figure out of a Longfellow poem – "the thoughts of youth are long, long thoughts." You could cast off the pier at Cliff Island and catch a mackerel, if you were lucky. On Peaks Island there was the excitement of the frequent ferries. On Long Island there was human activity at a nearby general store, and one September afternoon a boatload of softball players arrived from Chebeague to take on the indigenous Long Island team.

I wanted to play, but only watched and thought long thoughts until it was time to go.

At Chandler's Cove on those quiet fall Saturday afternoons, memories resonated from deep in my ten-year-old mind. I tried to recapture that moment – six or seven years before in adult-time, but several eternities hence in child-time – of clambering on the barnacled rock beside the wharf. Across the cove, on Indian Point, almost to the sandbar, a huge tree with an umbel-like top stood silhouetted in a way that seemed to me remote and wistful. *What kind of exotic tree is that?* I wondered for a long, long time.

* * *

When I gazed in 1980 from the little writing alcove on the Eastern Prom toward the smokestacks of the recently activated Wyman Unit 4, that tree still vibrated strong in memory. A year later came that camping trip when some friends and I rode the ferry to Chandler's Cove, trekked with backpacks over the barnacled rock to the beach and then along the boulder-clogged low-tide shore to Indian Point, where stood the tree itself. It was, of all things – after half a lifetime of thinking it may have been transplanted from a tropical isle – an oak. We walked the unkempt paths on Little Chebeague, camped under another ancient, spreading oak on the west end of the island, and encountered ticks.

Now both Chebeagues had locations and springs of memory.

Septembers in the late 1970s and early '80s, Biff Lea, the president of Tower Publishing Company where I tied my painter in Portland for eleven years, took the staff for an annual outing at the Chebeague Inn on the other end of the island from Chandler's Cove. We drove out to Cousins Island on sunny Saturday mornings and caught the ferry at the landing there. On all of these excursions, a remembrance echoed in of a moment sometime in the late 1950s when we had piled off Smitty's boat, it must have been, and into cars parked near the landing where we got hopelessly, surreally stuck in the mud. Angry men, the first time I saw boards used for traction under spinning tires, mud everywhere and in our shoes. Get out of the way! I guess we got out, but I don't know how.

I never mentioned it to my Tower co-workers, and never mentioned while we waited in the bare little shed at the end of the Cousins Island pier that I had spent innumerably long autumn afternoons with nothing to do there while the seaplane circled, landed, took off, circled and landed.

> I remember the gleams and glooms that dart
>> Across the school-boy's brain;
> The song and the silence in the heart,
> That in part are prophecies, and in part
>> Are longings wild and vain.
>>> And the voice of that fitful song
>>> Sings on, and is never still:
> "A boy's will is the wind's will,
> And the thoughts of youth are long, long thoughts."

There are thoughts you cannot utter without unspeakable complication. When we got to the Stone Wharf with fall jackets over our arms and day packs and sunglasses, and walked up toward the inn – dignified old 1920s structure – and the expanse of September grass where our cookout and lawn games were set up, I didn't try to explain to my friends I was actually, when you came right down to it, not visiting, but home. There were by then too many different springs of memory to talk about.

From the time of those September outings and the view from the Prom to the Unit 4 smokestacks to now, is an expanse of thirty-five years or so, the better part of an adult lifetime. The tide is in and separates them; the sandbar we walked has gone beneath the water. The recollections are like islands or nodes in time, connected underneath another expanse of water on the way to October of 1955.

The physicists say the arrow of time travels in one direction only. The past is irretrievably behind.

But Einstein clarified that, contrary to appearances, time is not a flow: It's a dimension. The October field, the Indian Point tree (gone now), the shuffle of horseshoe crabs, the throb of diesel engines, a fisherman and his mythic ship – they all have locations, like distant islands. This is a fact of physics.

For unknown reasons, the time dimension seems to be in motion and events are capturable only once. But the feelings in them resonate forever, like sound waves that dissipate but never vanish.

Somehow the tides of time divide us from the fathomable past. And then beneath, like vibrations up and down invisible strings, autumns past are in reality connected to the unfathomable spring of now, and on.

Periwinkle Voyages

Our routines long ago stopped taking us down to the fresh ruffles of the surf very often, but somehow, the sea is always with me nonetheless. There were ancient daylong excursions digging and scattering sand on Chandler's Cove and other beaches in Casco Bay, Cape Elizabeth and Scarborough. And more often, I malingered around low-tide pools and algae baking on damp ledges and poked around under wharves funky with kelp and bait smells.

Down in that gloomy intertidal no-man's-land, periwinkles were everywhere. They dotted the rocks and pilings, inhabited the seaweed. To a kid they were as motionless as stones and practically inanimate, even though you knew they were alive. Six or eight of them might be arrayed in a trapezoidal shape on a flat spur of ledge, then if you wandered away and later returned, the trapezoid had turned into a U. How did they do that, and when?

Barnacles don't move at all. They cement their heads directly onto the rock and stay there. But periwinkles suction themselves to flat surfaces at their shell aperture and shove one foot out to push around, typical of gastropods – a class of mollusks with spiral shells. Periwinkles have soft bodies and a head inside the permanent univalve shell (as opposed to bivalve like clams, scallops and mussels). South of New England there are tremendous varieties of periwinkle kin, from whelks, cowries, conchs and murexes, to wentletraps, tritons and augers. Don't ask me to identify these creatures I've mostly only read about and have no karmic links to. That I know of.

The three main periwinkle species I had a firsthand relationship with as a kid look a lot alike: the common periwinkle (Littorina littorea); the rough periwinkle (L. saxatilis); and the smooth periwinkle (L. obtusata). The common periwinkle has a purple-brown shell, with fewer color variations than the others. The rough periwinkle has deeper ridges in the shell. And the smooth periwinkle tends to look shinier and is often banded and brighter-colored in green and yellow.

Littorina littorea, believe it or not, is an invasive species. The first report of its presence in North America was near Pictou, Nova Scotia, in the 1840s. They appear to have come from Ireland and Scotland, according to a genetic study led by University of Maine marine biologist Susan Brawley, probably on ballast rock picked up in Britain and discharged in the Maritimes. Or possibly they were deliberately transplanted for food. They expanded their new range rapidly, and are now found from Labrador south to Delaware on a boost from a later introduction along the mid-Atlantic, in addition to their original digs on Northern Europe's coasts.

For food, they scrape algae off rocks and seaweed with a tooth-riddled contraption called a radula, which sticks out of the same aperture as the foot. There are so many of them off our coast that they sometimes devour the competitors of Irish moss, which then takes over in places, disrupting the ecosystem. Life is hazardous in the intertidal zone, and even nastier as you cross the line into the deeper water where their larger cousins the whelks are outright scavenging carnivores.

Periwinkles have organs to taste their food, as well as feel and smell, and they somehow hear, or at least detect, sound waves: It is apparently an astonishing fact that humming a tune can induce one to open its operculum, or aperture cover. I've never tried this, but have been assured by eyewitnesses it does indeed happen. Are periwinkles, aka snails, so civilized they recognize music?

No matter. In Europe and Asia, people still eat them, and they've been harvested for those markets by Down East "wrinklers" in considerable quantities since about the late 1980s. One year nearly 4 million pounds were taken. In the early decades of the 2000s the harvest has approached about 1 million pounds a year, according to Maine state figures.

Unless you crush a periwinkle or bore a hole in its shell, the tight-sealed aperture is the only way into it. Years ago, a friend who studied nutritional self-sufficiency experimented with collecting periwinkles on the shore in Portland and boiling them. They're easier to gather than clams, but eating them turns out to be labor-intensive. The cooked periwinkle meat is hard to dig out without breaking the shell and getting bites full of shards. Unless you're a green crab, which painstakingly crushes them in its great claw, and discards the bits.

I relate all this gathered-up information from one sort of distance or another. For as I say, we don't make many voyages to the shore nowadays and I don't have the same consanguinities with periwinkles that I have with, say, chickadees. So the fascination goes back to chthonic memories, bleached by time and the elements, of shell shucks under low-tide wharves, when it barely registered to me that they were even alive. They were small creeping stones with trap doors.

In the intertidal gloom under the wharf, across the terminator from sun-beaten day, it never occurred to me you could gather up periwinkles and do something as useful as eat them, the way they were eating algae, and algae were eating sunlight. To me they were just more bait. It takes the better part of the whole voyage to realize how cruel the bottom of the sea really is. And no one can tell you.

Autumnal Tints

In the first week of September, most years, come the days we wait all winter and, frankly, half the summer for. Slanting transparent-gold sunlight, warm chill air, blue sky, Canada geese, leaf and acorn scents.

It's the most gorgeous weather anywhere in the world. Anywhere I've been, at least. Here in northern New England it starts to gain maturity in mid to late July, like a great blue heron rising out of a stand of cattails and angling over the woods in the direction of October. One afternoon the sky is suddenly bluer than you remember it being all summer. The air is clearer, and the clouds seem purer white than anything you saw in, say, May. Goldenrod is everywhere, an emblem of time. Umbels of Queen Anne's lace bob like white moons over fieldsides. In August humidity and overcast sometimes haze the air, but that's a prelude to a September brightness that takes over everything and stuns your whole mood into a state of awakening.

October is the time of painted leaves, Thoreau said, and observed in his essay "Autumnal Tints" that it didn't always look like this, at least in our eyes. "The autumnal change of our woods has not made a deep impression on our literature," he wrote in 1856. "A great many who have spent their lives in cities, and have never chanced to come into the country at this season, have never seen the flower, or rather ripe fruit, of the year." He means the purple grasses, red maples, elms in "great brownish-yellow masses, warm from their September oven," and the fallen leaves themselves, which he calls "the acme of the Fall" in mid-October.

That was then, this is now, when the "leaf-peepers" (a literary phrase, if there ever was one) travel north even from Massachusetts to catch the October color. It was Thoreau who coaxed them out. He (along with Emerson and their Transcendentalist friends) taught us to look at the autumn woods: "There is just as much beauty visible to us in the landscape as we are prepared to appreciate – not a grain more." We almost literally owe autumn to him.

In recent years it has pushed further into October and even November than it did in his time. The trees calculate closing time by the shifting length and angles of daylight, which are the same as they were in the 1850s, but also by some sylvan measure of temperature. The acme of color in central Maine now is around early to mid-October, as it was in the 1800s in Thoreau's Concord, Massachusetts, 2 degrees of latitude or so farther south. It seems to me frosts strike later here than they did even thirty years ago, never mind two centuries ago in Massachusetts. Which if you ask me is practically tropical compared to Maine.

From one point of view, this is probably a sign of an unwelcome change in overall climate. But from another view, it's a stretching out of the time we wait for all year. There are afternoons in October, when the air is still and the Sun is angling across banks of grass, withering goldenrod and leaf-strewn athletic fields, where the whole of natural time seems to crystallize. You feel like the day has converged with every gorgeous fall day that ever was and Thoreau will come traipsing out of the woods with a red maple leaf in his hand that he raises in greeting.

It doesn't quite happen, of course. At least, not like that. But if your mind takes a certain angle, the echoes catch in the clear air and the leaves.

Night Flight

Suspended over the fir trees out my front door late-summer evenings is Altair. It's the brightest in a flat diamond of stars poised at an oblique angle over the trees, making up part of the constellation Aquila.

It's also one of the three bright stars in what's called in recent times the Summer Triangle: Altair, Deneb and Vega. To see the triangle around 9 or 10 p.m. in August, look toward the top of the sky – the brightest thing you see is Vega. Sweep left, and the star not quite as bright as Vega is Deneb. Altair toward the southern horizon is the apex of the equilateral triangle.

For quite a long time, the stars in this part of the sky have been associated with birds, or so the scholars indicate.

The name Altair comes from a phrase in the seventh- or eighth-century Arabic name for the constellation, Al Nasr al Ta'ir, the Flying Eagle, and means roughly "the rising one." The Babylonians and Sumerians three thousand years or more ago probably called it the Eagle Star, as did the Greeks later on. Aquila is Latin for eagle, from Roman times. The easily visible star just above Altair is Tarazed, and dimmer just below it is Alshain, both from an ancient Persian name for the whole asterism, Shahin tara zed, meaning in one translation "the star-striking falcon." Anyway it's an image of sweeping avian power in the stars.

Aquila still flies there summer nights above the treetops in central Maine. And higher to the east is Cygnus, the Swan, an easily spotted cross of six stars. Deneb is the top of the cross and the tail (al dhanab, in Arabic) of the swan. The central star is Sadr, the breast, and the lower star of the cross piece is

Gienah, from the Arabic al janah, "the wing" of the swan, or of the Hen for Arab astronomers. The Greeks also called the constellation Cycnos, the Swan, and simply Ornis, the Bird. Whatever you name it, the grace is unmistakable.

Near the zenith on August and early September nights is Vega in the constellation Lyra, the Lyre, with one of the oldest continuously used star names from Arab sources. Indigenous Arab people called it Al Nasr al Waqi, variously translated as "the eagle the falling one," or "the swooping eagle (or vulture)," or also "stone eagle of the desert." The word Vega after a millennium of use seems to derive from waqi. The Romans called the constellation the Lyre, and the bird and music imagery had been synthesized by the time Galileo turned telescopes skyward around 1610. The blue beauty of Vega, like a large bird in flight or like music, or both, is a force of grace and harmony in the sky.

For being stationary, these powerful birds reflect kaleidoscoping wheels of motion, and they're not alone. Shot from the bow of the archer Sagittarius – who is low on the horizon (behind my firs) in these parts during July and August – and flying on a trajectory that has missed the eagle and will in some mythic future just miss the swan, is the arrow, Sagitta. Its trajectory skirts Scutum, the Shield, where one of the most graceful of all star clusters dots the sky (also obscured by trees at my house), known in the 1700s as M11 and later the Wild Duck Cluster. In a small telescope it looks, if your mind rises to its level, like a distant flock of ducks scattering, or so W.H. Smyth thought in the 1800s. The feel of it, at least, mirrors the other powerful flight taking place in the summer stars.

The ancient astronomers couldn't see the Wild Duck Cluster, having no telescopes. And the truth is, the only constellation of all those named here whose dots connect to an image anything like its name is Cygnus. Even then, what we see there literally at a glance is a cross, not a swan. But like everything else in life, the more you watch the triangle of Aquila, Deneb and Vega, the more meets the eye. A lot more.

Even though they're fixed, these stars are in a special kind of flight relative to the season and the pointed firs. It's not just that they're enormous nuclear furnaces – so are the stars of Orion and the Big Dipper. These are a revelation of some cosmic motion that inspires a peculiar kind of awe. The awe you feel is your detection of invisible motion. An underlying motion, like powerful birds on the wing at night.

Kochab North

North of us every night, the handle of the Little Dipper is bending around from Polaris to the stars Pherkad and Kochab on the edge of its bowl. These two stars were referred to in ancient times as "the Guardians of the Pole," whose exact point is marked nowadays within about a degree by Polaris.

Kochab is an interesting star. (As if any star could ever be *un*interesting.) It's the brighter of the two guardians, at magnitude 2.08. (Pherkad is 3.05 – the higher the number, the dimmer the star.) It's about one hundred twenty-six light-years from us, reddish to the eye on clear nights, and redder still in binoculars, since it's a red giant – preparing for the end of its long life.

The Romans referred to Kochab and Pherkad as the Circlers, or Leapers, or Dancers around the pole, since the bowl of the Little Dipper wheels around Polaris once a year, and inside that yearly circle, a nightly circuit too, like layers of a dance.

Kochab's name is of uncertain origin. It may come from the Arabic Rucaba, which in the middle ages was the name of another, dimmer star in the constellation, or from the Arabic word "kaukaba," meaning star. It may also have been called, in Arabic, Al Na'ir al Farkadain, meaning the brighter of the two calves – the other calf being Pherkad, a shortened version of Farkadain.

Further into antiquity, the Greeks called it Polos, or Polar Light, and astronomers to the east identified it as the "mill peg." "The heavens there turn around in the way a millstone does," wrote the Greek astronomer Cleomedes around 300 B.C. The mill peg epithet for Kochab could be explained in part by the fact that around 1100 B.C., it actually was nearer true north than Polaris.

The stars, in other words, take slow turns marking true north because the Earth wobbles on its axis, like a top wobbling as it spins. One round of this wobble – known as precession – occurs about every twenty-six thousand years, during which the North Pole, at the top of the axis, slowly points out a great circle in the northern sky. For now the top of the Earth points almost exactly at Polaris. About three thousand years ago it pointed roughly at Kochab.

The ancient starwatchers had a kind of patience that I think is largely unknown nowadays. European, Arab, Roman, Greek, Egyptian, Babylonian and other adepts tracked starlight meticulously night in and night out for a long time, since at least three thousand years ago and probably much, much longer. They taught what they saw across generations, and some scholars think stargazers as long as seven thousand years ago – and likely more – were encoding what they saw happening in the sky into mythological stories. It seems clear, anyway, that by the time writing was first invented around five thousand to six thousand years ago, there was enough knowledge of celestial motions to construct astronomically aligned stone rings similar to Stonehenge, which was first built around four thousand seven hundred years ago. There's evidence in Germany of similar rings two thousand years before that.

Part of the mythological coding is this image of cosmic millstones turning in the sky and grinding out time. But the stone of the Great Year was slipping, up there. Its central peg wheeled slowly out of joint every so often in twenty-six thousand year cycles, wandering into cosmic catastrophe by flood or flame and with one peg replacing another. Every star eventually veered slowly from center.

In the fall, seen from the driveway in Troy, Kochab flickers rustily up there by the chimney. Just west of it is Thuban, which was in Polaris's place about the time of the building of Stonehenge and the Egyptian pyramids. Farther west is brighter Vega, which twelve thousand years from now will be within 5 degrees of where Polaris is now.

The stars look very steady from our little lifetime. But they're like this for just a moment or two, really. The whole sky grinds on whether we're there to watch or not, and takes us with it, every moment. If it's not now, it is to come. If it's not to come, then it will be now. If not now, yet it will come. The readiness is all, and the patience, which are guardians of the mind.

A Backyard Cosmography

On fall nights Hercules is tumbling shoulder-first toward the woods.

To find him, you look for Vega, which is west of overhead in September evenings. A bit farther west, approaching the horizon, there's an Arkansas-shaped trapezoid of four stars, which is the Keystone of Hercules. In myth imagery, this is his torso, basically upside down, or head over heels from our frame of reference. In ancient times this figure was known as the Kneeler. Later, in Roman times, it came to be called Hercules.

Extending from each of the four joints of the Keystone are stars that outline his arms and legs. At roughly the top, a knee is pinning the head of Draco, the Dragon, whom Hercules killed to get the golden apples of the Hesperides, the original daughters of darkness.

Off the lower part of the Keystone are his shoulders. The magnitude 2.8 star off the lower right corner is known as Kornephoros, which means "club bearer." Off the left, or southmost corner is Sarin, slightly dimmer at 3.2 magnitude. Hercules is said to be raising his club with his right arm extending from Kornephoros, and wearing his lion skin over his left arm, extending from Sarin. Past his shoulders, this star imagery is kind of hard to pick out.

In astronomy-speak, Sarin is a blue-white subgiant star. In fact, it's not one star at all, but two stars closely in line with each other. They're not connected gravitationally, but separate stars coincidentally in our line of sight. Anyway, in simplified scientific descriptions it's one star, relatively close to us seventy-nine light-years away.

A Backyard Cosmography

Sometime decades ago, Sarin became my main point of orientation in the summer sky. I can't remember how or when this happened. On June evenings it's high enough in the east to see over my firs, and all summer I watch it trail slowly westward. By nightfall in late October it has dropped behind my western tree line. All winter I wait for it to return.

On clear nights in August and September, I always stop to look at it, either sidelong while I'm walking up the driveway, or through binoculars or my little backyard telescope.

When I casually look up, Sarin has a weird way of disappearing in my eyes' blind spot. I guess there must be something unusual about its light, because to see it, I have to look at it peripherally. Most other stars don't pose this problem. With Sarin, the further my gaze averts, the more I see, but the less directly the light strikes my eye. It's a dusty-looking, very pale yellowish fire. In binoculars it hardens into a direct gem-spray like all stars seen through a lens, and in the telescope, it's a white, lonely, faintly icelike crystal.

It's a disquieting, yet familiar kind of light. To my mind, the known sky maps outward from Sarin.

And yet, even though it's the central peg of my own backyard cosmography, beyond marking Hercules' left shoulder Sarin has no story of its own. The origin of its name is unknown. As far as the star etymologists can figure, the word "Sarin" first appeared in the Skalnate Pleso star atlas created about seventy years ago by the Czech astronomer Antonin Becvar. But where Becvar got it (along with eleven other strange, untraceable names), no one knows. The Skalnate Pleso, which sounds like a phrase out of a science fiction novel, is the astronomical observatory in Slovakia where Becvar worked.

Your imagination of course can run wild with fantasies on Becvar's possible channels of information, given what regular exposure to starlight can do to your mind. Sarin has appeared to me in dreams with dazzling, dusty brightness. I've also envisioned it as a steady white combustion partly obscured by a disk of dust. No disk, however, has been detected by astronomers.

I wonder what it's like in the vicinity of Sarin. Since at least Plato's time, and apparently much longer, people's imaginations have been gripped by the sense that our origins are in the stars. Even now some scientists think life came to Earth on comets. In Plato's myth, the fixed stars were created originally as divine, eternal beings. Then when we sentient beings were created, each soul was assigned to a star. Sentient beings, he says, are in a process of being born into material bodies on Earth. Those who live well return to their stars of origin. Those who do not live well suffer ... a return to Earth.

It's hard to believe, as the biologist Lewis Thomas observed late last century, that a structure as complex as consciousness would simply dissolve, as though it had never existed. Nature just does not abandon complex structures like that. It tends to transform them, like ice crystals transforming into water or supernova jetsam transforming into stars. Or starlight transforming into dreams.

Almost everything that's happening out among the stars is completely and utterly unseen by human beings. The only clues come from their light. Once it hits the back of your retina and generates signals, you have to wonder what they are and try to place them, somehow. As scientific spectral readings and then interpretations of the data, or as dreams and then interpretations of the images. Something tells me there is a conflation of the two both far out and in deep.

A Backyard Cosmography

I wonder if I will get back to Sarin, and what it will look like, and what its name will be.

M31 and the Limits of Visibility

Clear as a bell over the treetops northeast of my backyard on August and September evenings rises the lopsided W of Cassiopeia. If you trace the line formed by the third and fourth stars from left to right and continue on roughly southeasterly, your eye runs into a large box of four stars, known as the Square of Pegasus. The brightest of those four stars, the one your eye runs straight into coming out of Cassiopeia, is Alpheratz, which despite being in the Square is actually the alpha star in the constellation Andromeda.

However, none of this is of any further interest. I'm just trying to get you oriented to what's coming.

A little more than halfway from Cassiopeia to Alpheratz on a clear night with no lights around, dip your eye down a bit. If you're patient you'll pick up a faint white smudge, just at the limit of visibility because it's so diffuse. With binoculars you can see it pretty easily.

It's the Andromeda galaxy, or M31 as stargazers refer to it. It's the only large galaxy visible by naked eye from Earth, and the largest galaxy in our Local Group of more than thirty galaxies within a volume of space about ten million light-years in diameter. The Large and Small Magellanic Clouds are also members of the Local Group, much smaller than M31 and the Milky Way, but bright and striking in the Southern Hemisphere because they're so much closer – one hundred and seventy-nine thousand and two hundred and ten thousand light-years away.

Dimensions: The Milky Way where we live is a spiral-shaped assembly of one hundred billion to four hundred billion stars (or possibly more, depending on which astronomer's estimate you use). It spans about one hundred thousand light-years across. We live about three-fifths of the way from the center in one of the arms, and are trundling along with billions of other stars around the center – which is anchored by at least one supermassive black hole – about once every two hundred and twenty million years or so.

M31 is a somewhat larger, less compact version of the Milky Way. It spans about two hundred and fifty thousand light-years and may have as many as a trillion stars. You'd think a clump of that many stars would be pretty bright in the sky, but of course M31's faintness results from its more or less incomprehensible distance: It's somewhere between 2.4 million and 2.9 million light-years from us. Its apparent magnitude is 3.4, but its wispiness makes it more elusive to your eye than a single star of roughly the same magnitude, like Sarin in Hercules or Thuban in Draco.

But once you've trained your eye to find it, M31 works a certain magnetic effect on your mind. At least, for me, I can't look into the fall sky without marking Cassiopeia, tracing the line through Andromeda to Alpheratz, and flipping slowly down until I come onto it. Often I don't catch it immediately, and have any number of times stalled my wife's schedule of events by going back inside to get the binoculars so I can seize the night.

It's awesome when you glimpse its chalky shape, unsettling when you focus long enough to sort out parts (the center is much brighter than the outer wisps), wider yet as your eye picks up more and more of its 2.5 million-year-old photons, and after a while it can send transmissions of cosmic fear up your spine and into the core of your brain where unutterably deep affinities process. Almost like you had lived there once and were recognizing home. Or something.

Something too much of this.

But it's not to say the impulses born from such feelings are unscientific exactly. If M31 is so much like the Milky Way, then why wouldn't there be watchers there too? And in fact, serious scientists (here, at least) have studied, for example, infrared light from M31 and other galaxies trying to get clues about the existence of extragalactic supercivilizations.

The basic framework of their search is what's called the Kardashev scale. Nikolai Kardashev is a Russian astronomer who in 1964, before Carl Sagan made talk of the possibility of intelligent extraterrestrial life publicly respectable, devised a way to talk about and detect the presence of such civilizations. In his paper "Transmission of Information by Extraterrestrial Civilizations" (published in *Soviet Astronomy-AJ*, Vol. 8 No. 2, Sept.-Oct. 1964), Kardashev summarized his idea like this:

> In line with the estimates arrived at, it will prove convenient to classify technologically developed civilizations in three types:
>
> I – technological level close to the level presently attained on the earth, with energy consumption at ~4 x 1019 erg/sec.
>
> II – a civilization capable of harnessing the energy radiated by its own star (for example, the stage of successful construction of a "Dyson sphere"); energy consumption at ~4 x 1033 erg/sec.
>
> III – a civilization in possession of energy on the scale of its own galaxy, with energy consumption at ~4 x 1044 erg/sec.

In other words, alien civilizations might be detectable according to how they derive and use energy resources from their planet (Type I), their home star (Type II), or their whole galaxy (Type III).

In 2015, a group of astronomers affiliated with The American Astronomical Society reported they had surveyed about one hundred thousand nearby galaxies, based on the hypothesis that: "Nearby Type iii (galaxy-spanning) Kardashev supercivilizations would have high mid-infrared ... luminosities." They did not find any behaviors of mid-infrared light suggesting the presence of supercivilizations, but they did note "90 poorly understood sources and 5 anomalous passive spirals [that] deserve follow-up via both SETI and conventional astrophysics."

Is there intelligent – or superintelligent – life on some fabulous Earth-like planet orbiting a star in the Andromeda galaxy? The probability calculations have of course been made in many different ways, but as the evidence that most stars have planets piles up, it starts to seem less and less likely that there isn't other intelligence somewhere in our galaxy of a hundred billion stars, never mind M31 with a trillion possible systems. While M31 is so far away that trying to see one of its planets is like trying to get a hydrogen atom in focus with a pair of binoculars, still, some astronomers a few years ago observed starlight behaviors there that led them to cautiously suggest they had evidence of the first extragalactic planet. What are the chances.

This is all coming out of this wisp of light, the least of lights you can see on autumn nights. A smudge that must have been noticed in ancient times when city lights weren't washing out the sky – though puzzling to me is the fact that the first recorded mention of the Andromeda galaxy does not appear until the year 964 in the *Book on the Constellations of the Fixed Stars* by Abu I-Husain al-Sufi, in which he depicts it as a large fish lying across the constellation Andromeda as it was drawn eight centuries earlier by his predecessor Ptolemy. Why didn't Ptolemy, the great astronomical authority for fifteen hundred years, mention it? He must have seen it, there. What did he think he was seeing?

To al-Sufi and Ptolemy and all the astronomers up through the nineteenth century, this smudge of light would have been a "nebula," or cloud beyond the earthly clouds. They had no idea the universe was any bigger than the solar system until telescopes started to slowly crack open the problem of size in the seventeenth and eighteenth centuries. And the fact is, it hasn't even been a hundred years (as of this writing) since Edwin Hubble determined there are galaxies beyond our galaxy.

In 1920, the idea that the universe contained "island universes" had been around for more than a century, but there was no proof of it. The Milky Way appeared to be all there was of everything. The Andromeda galaxy was described as a nebula of some kind, possibly a cloud of stars within the Milky Way. But Hubble in the early 1920s observed light in M31 behaving the same way the light from stars called Cepheid variables behaves. These stars – named for the constellation Cepheus where the first one was noticed – pulsate in regular ways at predictable brightnesses, which gives astronomers enough information to calculate their approximate distances. Hubble's observations revealed that the Cepheid variables in M31 were way beyond the edge of the Milky Way. M31 was a whole other galaxy.

Hubble in 1923 figured the distance as nine hundred thousand light-years, but as telescopes improved and data were collected through the twentieth century and into the twenty-first, the calculations improved and now the estimates indicate a distance of somewhere between 2.4 million and 2.9 million light-years.

* * *

This trillion stars, millions of light-years away, looks like a wisp only for now, mind you. As more light-data came in, it was observed that M31 is actually moving toward us. And in the mid-2010s some astronomers projected their scientific vision into the far future and found it's likely the Milky Way and the Andromeda galaxy will collide some four billion years from now.

What will that look like, here on Earth? That just-visible wisp of light in, say, five hundred million years might be like a bright star only larger. In a billion years it will be brighter and larger still, with a hair-raising elliptical symmetry slashing angle-upward in the sky. In two billion years, it dominates the horizon. Approaching four billion years from now, it's filling autumn evenings – if such things still exist – looming like the gigantic, terrifying face of an angel.

If any humans are left, I mean. By then the Sun will be entering its old age phases and getting ready to expand. Our constellations will have long since dissolved, because the stars will have made more than seventeen circuits around the galactic center and wandered away from the areas we see them now. Meanwhile, as the two galaxies dance slowly closer, gravity on a galactic scale will start to upset everything. The planets will likely be thrown off their orbits, and that could mean anything for planet Earth and whatever form life might be taking then. Another four billion years of evolution might well have swept us straight through our own Kardashev incarnations and merged us with the others.

Somehow I doubt it's anywhere near that simple, though. All you can do is project your momentary mind forward to the same familiar line of firs and pines, the same affinity for starlight. In the year Three Billion, whole different

147

constellations make their annual circuits and M31 is enormous in the northeast. It's a spectacular cloud of diamonds and nebulae spilling upward halfway through the arms of the Milky Way. When another billion gradual years elapse, it's merged and turned the sky to a white sheet of stars, re-shaping again and again the upper limits of visibility.

Lunar Eclipse

Unsure whether I'd ever be awake for such an event again, I placed the Earth-based 4.5-inch Newtonian reflecting telescope on the deck and aligned it to the cardinal directions, unpacked a lens filter for moonlight, hung a pair of binoculars around my neck and aimed a lawn chair strategically south one September evening to watch the total lunar eclipse transpire in full, perfect view above my spruces and pines.

It was my third encounter with a total lunar eclipse. One I watched from an attic window on Munjoy Hill in 1982 with a blanket around my shoulders, a notebook (long lost) and an astronomy textbook. The next I watched from the campus of the State University of New York in Binghamton in 1993, and spent most of those couple of hours talking about China and the size of the cosmos with two friends.

The eclipse of September 2015 was different, not only for being in the quiet woods instead of a city, but also for being decades along in my ability to make sense out of what I was seeing. I find the whole thing more shadowy than ever.

The mechanics of a lunar eclipse – which is what I thought I was experiencing the first two go-rounds – are pretty simple, really. The Earth is orbiting around the Sun, and the Moon orbits around the Earth roughly once a month. (You can see the ghost of the word Moon in the word month.) When the Earth's orbit takes it directly between the Sun and Moon, then the Moon passes through the Earth's shadow, and is eclipsed.

It happens only when the Moon is full because that's when it's directly opposite the Sun. The reason there isn't a lunar eclipse every month is that the Moon's orbit is angled about 5 degrees to the plane of the Earth's orbit of the Sun. So the Moon's orbit takes it through the Earth's shadow only when the orbits combine at the appropriate angles. Sometimes the Moon passes through the edge, or penumbra, of the Earth's shadow producing a penumbral eclipse, or it brushes the edge of the central shadow, or umbra, producing a partial eclipse.

I was thinking hard about these mechanics in 1982 and 1993, trying to place myself in a context with them. I couldn't do it, really. The whole spherical contraption is too big and only leads to even bigger perplexities, like solar eclipses (a lunar eclipse on Earth is a solar eclipse on the Moon) and the insignificance of the distance to Pluto (4 light-hours) when you compare it to the distance to the nearest star (4.2 light-years), never mind the nearest large galaxy (2.5 million light-years). (For the record, the distance from Earth's surface to the Moon is about 1.3 light-seconds.)

On the deck in the clear, chilly September evening, the full Moon is so bright it actually boggles your eyes in a telescope. The more so when they're wearing out anyway. So a filter on the lens cuts the glare. Craters, plains and mountain shadows, all white and gray. Soon a fuzzy convex darkness starts inching onto the Moon wafer. With cosmic patience you wait, look through the binoculars, get up for a closer view in the telescope. The binoculars are better, really, because while the telescope shows the surface details, the binoculars show the whole Moon suspended deep in space.

As darkness swells slowly across the Moon's surface, it turns reddish, not black. The Moon is still reflecting indirect light and the Earth's atmosphere filters out the blue wavelengths, letting the reddish light through. September's vanishing Moon did not appear as red as the other two eclipses. At least in memory, which has a way of transforming things.

As the shadow increases, moonlight fades, of course, and the sky finds its off-phase dark. Stars that were invisible a little while ago emerged all over. Soon I could see the galaxy in the northeast. A few meteors streaked the sky, a couple of them bright. Eventually, inevitably, totality approached. The world was a reddish-dark orb suspended over the woods.

Down on the edge of the deck, a tiny point of light appeared. What the heck is that? It shone steadily for a minute or two. When I raised the binoculars to look at it, which would have done no good whatsoever, it winked out. All I could think of was the reflection from the back of a wolf spider's eyes. I've seen that before, and this glint on the deck was the right pinpoint size. But I don't know, and have no other rational explanation.

In the woods things moved around cracking branches like in a dream. Deer, probably. I don't know. Further back was the eight-note lyric wraith of a barred owl, often pronounced bard owl, and I suppose it is a poetry from an even deeper dark – *who cooks for you?*

Now and then a glint of starlight shot through the trees from outer space – when the rotating Earth aligns a clear shaft through maples and hemlocks, for a fleeting second a star at just the right angle on the skyline peeks through.

Maybe by that time I was only half-awake. The rusty Moon was suspended among the stars like a being in a dream.

Myths about eclipses usually depict some kind of conflict: a battle in the sky; displeasure among the gods; a portent of death; a sign of imbalance. Since we in our scientific wisdom know the mechanics of eclipses, we dismiss the mythologies as childish, if forgivable, nonsense. Scientists have long assumed and even teach that members of "primitive" cultures mistakenly believed the Moon is literally being attacked or eaten during an eclipse.

But assuming the myth makers believed the stories represent literal facts is as childishly mistaken about psychological reality as the stories are childishly mistaken about scientific reality. The Pomo Indians of the West Coast did not think the bear in their story literally attacked the Moon during a lunar eclipse, any more than we think the Sun literally rises in the morning.

Their story of the Moon and the bear conveyed, not facts of outer physical reality, but facts of inner psychic reality. In their cosmology, the difference between outer reality and inner reality was not as sharp as our Newtonian scientific cosmologies take it to be. The boundaries between woods and dreams, Earth and sky were wider and much more shadowy to them than they are to us. You might meet a bear in the woods, or you might meet him in a dream. They are identical beings in different versions of the world. In an eclipse on an abnormal evening in September, the bear that cracks branches in the woods crosses out of the dream and turns up as a shadow over the Moon. The physical world and the dream world intersect in the lunar world. "The sky is just the same as the Earth, only up above, and older," goes a translated observation from a Micmac story.

For a little while the rust-colored Moon hung suspended in deep space like a being in a dream. Sitting there on the deck in the trees while the Moon got eaten by a shadow, I awoke to at least a penumbra of the inner life. It was disturbing and I was haunted by thoughts of loved ones who seem to me these days in tangled woods, the path lost, old fears stirring, one in particular I was helpless to lead out. Conflict, imbalance, a heavy displeasure. The atmosphere of a lunar eclipse.

It took a couple of long hours of patient watching for the Earth's shadow to cover the whole white wafer. Science promised it would equally slowly uncover and return to its eye-boggling brightness. Somehow, there on the deck in the owl-hooting woods, it seemed sort of uncertain, though. Would it really return?

Of course it would. It's mechanically inevitable. But to make sure, I left the telescope standing and waited in my chair until a slip of light re-appeared on the edge of the Moon.

Thoreau, Poe and September

The first bite of fall in Troy usually comes in the first week or so of September. Just a slight tell-tale chill rolling through the kitchen window, like a nip on the ear. Birch leaves are strewing the deck, and the sumac has been reddening since August – it always gives in early, like a tropical-looking coward. The birds have picked the red osier clean of berries. Wasn't it just last week I was poking around in its flat white blossoms for signs of arachnid life (and hence, insect death)? Well, no, that was three months ago.

Technically the first week of September is still summer, since the Sun doesn't pass through the equinoctial plane until around the 22nd on its southward descent, not to return until the other side of next year. It sometimes happens nowadays that the first of September is sweltering. In case there's any doubt about how September weather trends, Thoreau on September 7, 1853, recorded 93 degrees in Concord, Massachusetts.

But he usually caught the first signs of fall in August: "The wind is autumnal and at length compels me to put on my coat," he wrote on August 12, 1854. And on August 26, 1856: "More wind and quite cold this morning, but very bright and sparkling, autumn-like air, reminding of frosts to be apprehended."

I remember a Labor Day long ago when having nothing else to do between the split shift of my handyman job at my cousin's country store in East Sebago, Maine, I drove up Route 114 to Naples to play golf by myself. I was worse at golf than any other sport I've stumbled through, slicing or hooking practically every try, and that day a gale was wheeling across the hills, trees and fairways, tossing my already-errant ball like a leaf. Huge clouds with dark gray undersides rolled overhead. Behind them, a cobalt blue sky. A November-like chill bit through my jacket. On one green I wished for gloves. Now, more than forty years later, that day is as crisp and intense to me as a new apple. Its bite and cool form a touchstone to my ur-image of precipitous fall.

Four days after the 93 degrees, Thoreau noted: "Cool weather. Sit with windows shut, and many by fires. … The air has got an autumnal coolness which it will not get rid of again. Signs of frost last night in M. Miles's cleared swamp. Potato vines black."

Well, if I am not mistaken, this timetable has in recent decades nudged further into the month. Even in central Maine, which has a couple of weeks' northeasterly lead toward winter over Massachusetts, mid-Octobers lately are often warm. My kidhood recalls mostly stark, clear, skinbiting, Poe-like air and shuffling oak and maple leaves. But in recent years here in Troy it's often been October before frost perched on the ground, and November before the meadow grass has turned full brown.

Nowadays most of us cherish the clear autumn chill and the color in the trees, but it wasn't always the case.

"Most [people]," Thoreau observed near the end of his life in 1862, "appear to confound changed leaves with withered ones, as if they were to confound ripe apples with rotten ones." The autumn leaves, he said, are signs of ripening rather than decay, and the red blazes in the maples are fruits, not signs of bitter death.

Still, there's no escape from the fact that the first September chill is the first breath of winter, so how do we find our bliss in that?

"The tone of the highest manifestation [of Beauty] … is sadness," Poe said with inverse, almost perverse razorlike accuracy. Maybe our love of cool air, withering grass and goldenrod, and falling leaves is a deep-set feel for the beauty in an ending.

As I put the finishing touches on this fumblesome little essay, a flock of geese went honking, flapping and racing on before the cold, directly over the house. They will not return, till much later.

The Auroras of Autumn

In those mysterious seasons when the world is twisting into or out of winter, the signal in the sky is the auroras, especially around the equinoxes. Disturbances in Earth's magnetic field are about twice as likely to occur at these times – why, the scientists do not know.

It's a phenomenon as strange, for now, to the scientific mind as to a backyard naturalist's eye. I've stood on the edge of a field near my house in Troy and watched auroras fill the sky – huge snakes of polar green kindling like ice and fire between me and the Big Dipper. They twist and seem to shimmer with tinges of blue and violet, then fade like thoughts into the cosmic background. Then re-emerge.

The farther north you go, the brighter and more enormous they are. You can only think how those huge cloud mountains running like water through waves of light might have played on the imagination of an ancient Wabanaki standing in a clearing. What did they signify?

The scientists explain the auroras like this: The Sun generates streams of electrically charged atomic particles called the solar wind. Some of the particles moving us-ward get trapped in the Earth's magnetic field, and they tend to flow toward the poles. There, they interact with other particles, energy is released, and arcs of green light, stupendous to our eyes, slowly bend and twist across the sky.

Around the autumn equinox, when the Northern Hemisphere has reached the halfway point between its full tilt toward the Sun in June and its full tilt away from the Sun in December, the auroras intensify. The same in spring. It has nothing to do with temperatures. It's thought that "rope-like magnetic connections" develop along the angle between the Earth and Sun, and more charged particles travel along those connections and channel toward the magnetic pole around the equinoxes. In turn, the Northern Lights intensify.

On the Sun, flares, prominences and ejections of material that amount to colossal explosions take place pretty frequently. Some of them are associated with sunspots, which increase and decrease in frequency over eleven-year cycles, and sometimes the explosions are so huge they disrupt radios and electric grids on Earth. The causes of the eruptions are not understood well enough to predict when they're going to happen in most cases. A few Septembers ago, right on the seasonal schedule, the space weatherologists reported a tremendous light show that was triggered by a coronal mass ejection that sent a huge cloud of charged particles streaking Earth-ward at more than three million miles per hour.

The Sun and Earth are invisibly connected – this much is known. Some of the connections reveal themselves from time to time as tremendous green serpents of light in the sky. And those connections intensify – for reasons not fully understood – just when summer and winter are haggling over March, which is the tipping point that signals summer will soon blaze up, as quick as a straw fire, or as an auroral substorm, or as a thought.

The auroras of autumn likewise pile on over the fields, the hills, the tinted distances of pine in the direction of the great closing down. What significance this has for me, or for an ancient Wabanaki, I have no idea.

The Most Brilliant of All Tangible Things

September and October are, of course, the perennial time of painted leaves. There are better years and worse years for color, but the red maple beside the driveway never misses. It's always one of the first to show fire, just as it's first to bud in spring, and every fall it blazes even when its fellow poplar, birch and ashes are simply fading to yellow.

No one is sure how to predict the intensity of the autumn tints. It's well-known that the principal sparks of leaf-flame are lessening light and cooling air. It also seems clear the weather – dry or wet, cloudy or sunny – affects the chemical changes in the leaves. So does the tree's location. But how these parts fit together, exactly, has not been scientifically established. Are the trees brighter after a wetter September, or after a drier one? Debatable and debated. And why this maple is so reliably the most brilliant of burning bushes among the chokecherry, raspberry, dogwood, birch and huge pine surrounding it, seems nigh-on inexplicable.

The leaves are green in summer because they're flush with chlorophyll, a pigment that soaks up light the tree uses to photosynthesize into energy. (To a tree, light is food.) Chlorophyll absorbs red and blue light, and reflects back green light, making the leaves green. Chlorophyll is a somewhat unstable compound, and so the tree has to manufacture it continuously all summer. To do this, it needs light and warmth.

At the tag end of summer, daylight dwindles, the Sun strikes less directly, and the air cools. It's harder for the tree to maintain its chlorophyll levels.

Meanwhile, the leaves contain other pigments as well. Carotene absorbs blue and blue-green light and reflects back yellow light, and anthocyanins absorb blue, blue-green and green light, and reflect back red. As the chlorophyll levels diminish, the carotene and anthocyanin levels stay the same or even increase, and so less green light, and more yellow and red light is reflected from the leaves. They turn red, yellow, orange, copper and purple according to the measures of carotene and anthocyanins in them. A red maple has a lot of carotene and its leaves turn scarlet. A sugar maple has more anthocyanin and its leaves show orange amid the red.

Because of the shorter periods of sunlight and the colder air, the deciduous trees gradually shut down their energy-making processes, and part of that shutdown includes shedding leaves. As the sunlight declines day by day, the production of growth hormones slows, and the leaves begin to age and die, a process called senescence. A layer of dead cells builds up between the leaf stem and the twig. Eventually that layer becomes brittle and breaks, and the leaf falls. A full-grown oak tree will shed a quarter of a million leaves.

How quickly a tree closes down its chlorophyll-manufacturing process has to do with variabilities of moisture, temperature and light, but no one knows a formula for it.

The red maple by our driveway apparently knows it, but reveals it in flames rather than explains it by equations. It is what it is, and somehow seems superior to the sum of its chemical parts. A revelation beats an explanation every time, in my book.

Beyond the Books

"What's this?" Bonnie said.

She held up a shiny, speckled red ball about the size of an acorn. Me being the backyard naturalist and science fictionist in the house, and everybody else being merely curious, she expected I'd have an answer, or at least a weird guess.

"I have no idea," I said. "Where did you get it?"

"Jack found it in the grass by the Shed."

She handed it to me. It was smooth and looked like some kind of fruit or nut, although it had no apparent stem end. I went outside to look around.

Around the Shed (which outside looks like a run-down toolshed, but inside is a library with wall-to-wall books) are fir, pine, beech, oak, maple, hemlock and cedar trees, none of which drops small round fruits. That I know of. The Shed is attached to the garage, the other side of which are a red-osier dogwood and the carcass of an elm tree that died so suddenly you'd swear it had a heart attack. But they don't grow acorn-sized fruit either. In fourteen years here in Troy, we'd never seen this thing before.

I searched the ground among the acorns. Soon I spotted one of the red fruits and picked it up. Weird. Were they a rare type of acorn? Or maybe they were pods of uncertain origin that would send out tendrils in the night, fasten themselves to our sleeping faces, and clone us into expressionless human-alien hybrids that would dispose of our withered bodies in Wednesday's trash.

Maybe not.

Back in the kitchen I got out the tree and flower books and paged through, but found nothing resembling the pods, as we were now calling them. I gave up for the time being and left them on the kitchen table, hoping the tendrils would not be long enough to reach the bedroom.

The next evening, the pods were noticeably drying out. Two days later they were downright shriveled, like oversized raisins. When I went back out to the Shed, where the science fiction novels actually are housed – out of range of those who are merely curious – I picked up five or six more pods and rechecked the tree and flower books – which are kept in the house itself – but still found no resemblances.

Next morning I brought a fresh, shiny one to the office. None of the other amateur botanists could identify it either. When a day later the pod was shriveling, one of my colleagues who knows a lot more biology than me decided to solve the problem before baby creatures with prehistoric teeth started erupting from our chest cavities while we worked.

The truth, as often happens, was one of those disturbing natural phenomena that generate, rather than result from, science fiction. It was not a fruit. It was a growth.

On a table in the office library, we cut the pod open. Inside was a white worm, or more accurately, a larva. The larva, we eventually discovered, was that of a gall wasp, a tiny nonstinging flying insect. The gall wasp laid its egg in an oak leaf and left a chemical that induced the tree to grow this fleshy pod, or gall, around the egg. The larva grew inside the gall and would feed on it. Some galls grow right inside the acorn, and some, like the ones around the Shed, grow outside and fall out of the trees.

When nature gets an idea, watch out. At least two hundred species of creatures use oak trees to make galls to nurture their young. Some birds and squirrels know they're there, and eat them.

Sometimes it seems uncomfortably like nature has an actual imagination. Nothing seems too weird for it, or too far off the beaten track – unlike most of us who don't stray too far from the house, lest the monsters make us mad.

An Old Bee

Beside the driveway one late-September morning, a bee with rust-colored midparts was poring over some New England asters, bright purple-blue-rayed medallions in tight clusters. He was making his way over each blossom, methodically prodding each dusky orange central disk, working very slowly to gather what nectar he could to make the honey that feeds the larvae in the nest. He did not seem inclined to search out more blossoms, but for as long as I watched him, he just worked the cluster he was on, making his way on foot from central button across petals to button.

No doubt it was fall that was slowing him down. He didn't have much longer to live, because the workers and drones of species Bombus ternarius all die before the snow flies. The young queens overwinter and build new nests in sheltered spots on the ground in springtime.

He crept from flower to flower. His fur was black-and-yellow-banded behind his head, with swaths of rust-orange on his abdomen, then yellow and black again near the tail. Smoky-colored wings folded over his back. His face and legs probed and gathered with dexterity and diligence. There was clearly intelligence at work. What that intelligence would be like is of course practically unknowable, but he moved with purpose and – do I overstep my own perceptions? – awareness of some kind. What is an old bee at the end of his working life aware of?

Suddenly my vision shifted and I was living in the bee's world. I saw into the aster disks, the scant sweet moisture there, and the maples, spruces and raspberry thicket a few yards away, the flowers and withered goldenrod were one intensely vivid, yawning, blank enormity. It was a completely fathomless wilderness, the way you'd feel if you had strayed from your little settlement on Mars, the only one, into the pointless red desert. Silent, trackless, stark and vacant. No memory, no path, no mental image, no art. It was utterly empty at its heart. It had no heart. Somewhere there was the nest. There was no word "forest" because a word would fill it.

I did not become the bee, as some naturalists, like Annie Dillard with her weasel, report, but simply stumbled over the edge into the bee's world and saw what he sees – saw it for a minute or two or maybe more, I don't know, until a few words bubbled into my mind telling me what I was seeing. With the appearance of the words my entry was lost, the empty woods receded, and I was back on the edge of the driveway observing the old bee diligently doing his job for maybe the final time. Whether he knew that or not, I have no idea.

Equinox Sunlight

Around the autumn equinox, sunlight in our part of the world, especially around dusk, takes on a clarity that seems practically supernatural. It makes a certain slant through birches, oaks and pines in ways unseen at any other time of year. In late afternoon the goldenrod skeletons and scarlet sumac and even stands of horseweed radiate energy that practically sets the day on fire.

Part of what's going on physically to create these effects on your bewildered, bedazzled autumn soul, I think, are the light's quick angles.

Toward the end of September (and of March) the Sun sets faster than it does at other times. Around the solstices (around June 21 and December 21) at our latitude (which in Troy is 44.6 degrees north), it takes roughly three and a half minutes from the moment the bottom of the Sun's disk first touches the western horizon to the moment the top of the disk disappears. At the equinoxes (around September 21 and March 21), it takes less than three minutes. This doesn't seem like much when you're just reading these numbers. But imagine standing there waiting. Like watching the pot come to a boil, time is contextual in your mind.

Why does the Sun set more quickly in September? The answer is that in September it's making an essentially vertical descent to the horizon. In June, it approaches the horizon at an angle.

The Earth is tilted on its axis with respect to the Sun. In other words, the North and South poles are tipped at an angle (of about 23.5 degrees) to the Sun. This tilt gives rise to the seasons. In the part of the orbit when the North Pole is tipped toward the Sun, the Sun climbs higher and stays up longer, and we have summer. In the part of the orbit when the North Pole is tipped away, the Sun is lower, the days are shorter, and we have winter. (This cycle is swapped in the Southern Hemisphere.)

In its course between its highest point in June and its lowest point in December, the Sun naturally crosses a midpoint. This happens in September and March, and is called the equinox. At that midpoint, the Sun sets due west, neither high toward the north (as in June) nor low toward the south (as in December). So when it's setting, it goes for all practical purposes straight down on the western horizon. The straight path, of course, is shorter and quicker than the path that angles down from north or south.

The word "equinox" is from Latin words meaning "equal" and "night," and the gist is that at the equinox, the hours of night are equal to the hours of daylight. But just as the longest and shortest daylight hours do not occur on the solstices, the days when light and dark hours are exactly equal (called the "equilux") do not occur on the equinoxes either. At our latitude, the equilux is a few days after the equinox. (We are talking about differences of less than a minute, here. See above: watched pot.)

Two factors influence this. One involves the way sunrise and sunset are calculated. Sunrise occurs, technically, at the moment the top of the Sun's disk appears on the eastern horizon. Sunset, technically, occurs the moment the top of the Sun's disk disappears on the western horizon. Now, the atmosphere is bending the Sun's rays. So in the morning, the rays are bending in over the horizon and the Sun is visible there for several minutes before its actual, physical disk breaks over the plane of the horizon. Similarly, at sunset, the Sun remains visible, with its rays bending back up over the horizon, for several minutes after the actual, physical disk has gone under the horizon. So the calculated time of sunset differs from the experienced time of sunset.

The second factor in the moveable date of equilux is that it does not suddenly become dark at the moment of sunset. Sunlight is still bending in through the atmosphere even after you've seen the Sun wink under the horizon; our experience of this air-bending light is twilight. Technically there are three kinds of twilight, according to *Dark Sky* diarist Steve Owens, and "dark" hours are calculated according to which of the three kinds of twilight you take to be still within a range you want to call daylight.

The three kinds of twilight are: civil twilight, when the Sun is up to 6 degrees below the horizon and enough light is still bending in to allow, say, a soccer game to continue; nautical twilight, when the Sun is 6 to 12 degrees below the horizon and most of us would say it's dark (like the referees who once ended a soccer game with the score 2-1, my son's team pressing – and forty seconds left on the clock), but sailors can still distinguish the horizon and take measurements from bright stars; and astronomical twilight, when the Sun is 12 to 18 degrees below the horizon, dark to us, but enough light still bends in to interfere with stargazing.

The exact moment of equinox is calculated at the moment the center of the Sun's disk crosses the midpoint in its north-south track. So the calculation of sunrise and sunset by the top of the Sun's disk and the twilight factor throw seconds and minutes of discrepancies between equinox calculations and equilux calculations.

In late September, the Sun is moving most quickly and directly toward the horizon. Its angles of light are transforming the landscape into a subtly turning kaleidoscope, to my eye at least.

Botanoluminescence

The angles of autumn sunlight bending in through clear September air, firing red and yellow leaves, seem to pry something invisible loose. Dry brown stalks and inflorescences of grass are illuminated as if from inside. Scarlet sumac and goldenrod skeletons and stands of horseweed radiate. The secret of time appears to be underneath these autumn angles, and how they seem to move and play, and unfurl things there in the field.

It takes superhuman patience to keep a scientific eye.

The red maples, copper beech leaves, purple grasses and burst milkweed pods become prisms of things unseen, directing otherwise invisible glints of divinity onto your retina and transforming them there, right in the same angle where the sea and Sun vanish into each other. In the crystal clear autumn sunlight, eternity is as near to tangible as it can get and not kill you. The day is on fire.

September Field

A September field that's so beautiful it's transfixing. Grasses in different shades of steel and emerald and crowds of yellowing milkweed running up a small slope. Fleabanelike white asters with round bluish stars and gold centers growing in clumps, in places child-high thickets. Sprays of late goldenrod are so yellow they practically vibrate, and the rest have stiffened into gray ghosts. Here and there are violet clusters of New England asters. Queen Anne's lace folded into greenish bird's nests and their sisters the hemlock parsley grow like sparse galaxies in the uncut brown interstices at the field margin. To the right are hay rolls, sweet-smelling even in the random distance. There's not a sound.

At the top of the rise, oaks and maples have a few rust and copper leaves and in another week will burst into flame. Birch leaves are turning dirt-saffron. Beyond the hay rolls green spruce spikes line the dirt road. Today, silver-gray clouds, almost globelike, roll overhead, and a great blue heron flaps soundlessly across. This beauty is so intense it's almost unendurable. It's something you only see in pictures.

•

The angel in Leonardo da Vinci's painting *Annunciation* stares at Mary with exactly this force. On one knee and raising two fingers in some cosmic signal, it gazes with supernatural firmity at Mary who seems entranced. The folds of Mary's dress seem as random as the hay rolls, but like the hay rolls, they're not. They're circling her knees and midsection. The angel itself is virtually whirling. Three circles just discernible to the eye – around bended knee and shoulder, upraised arm and wings (which a later painter retouched and discopernicated), and inside that, its head – are spinning there in outline. Between the two is a dark vanishing point where the angel's force meets Mary's stunned attention.

•

This field has stunned me. It's nature caught in the act of announcing itself. The asters and hemlock parsley are little starlike wheels. The hay rolls, yellowing milkweed and graying goldenrod are twisting into the distance before my eyes. Above them are the ballooning steel clouds. And in the extraterrestrial expanse beyond them, Jupiter will rise tonight, a little earlier than the night before, with its moons circling inside its round of the Sun. Beyond the planets' orbits the stars in Cassiopeia and Pegasus will also rise and Hercules will just again be setting in the wheel of the firmament that turns overhead year after year, season after season. These wheels grind away inside another, greater circuit of the stars around the Earth's pole every twenty-six thousand years, and they all whirl like clockworks inside yet a greater wheel they all travel around the galaxy every two hundred and fifty million years.

There's a story about a man who prayed to see an angel, and one revealed itself as a disk spinning three or four feet above the ground, maybe in a field like this one. Dissatisfied, he demanded to see the angel's real face. The angel told the man he shouldn't wish for such things, but the man persisted and the angel said, "Then look." The man screamed – the angel's face filled the sky, its gaze fixed unendurably on him. "Never let me see a sight like this again!" the man shouted.

There are angels this close to your face in this autumn field, and presumably in all fields, and everywhere else. I have no more idea what this means than the man who saw an angel in the sky. I only know this field here east of Unity has transfixed me, and this is what it is like.

No Butterflies

September. The goldenrod and asters glow in the hazy afternoon sunlight. The maple leaves already show signs of dryness.

On this side of the chain link fence around the basketball court, two yellow butterflies chase each other like errant electrons. Dart and kiss, light, drop, skip along the goldenrod. There's hardly a breath of wind. Humid sunlight streams like gold through the grass. The two clouded sulphurs flit and separate, one goes east, the other west toward the field. The east-moving wings swoop up then down, then back, and suddenly the chaotic yellow tandem pops together again, nips and flutters on beyond the cattails as if they were tethered on a string.

Are they mating? Or fighting? Or playing? Can butterflies play? What compels companionship airborne in minds so small?

It's not the wind blowing them in dancing tandem across the field. It might not be will exactly, either, since consciousness, according to many neuroscientists, doesn't even exist – your awareness is nothing more than biochemicals firing in not-yet-mapped, arcanely complex processes. You are not there.

And neither are the butterflies, when you come down to it. The humid air, the goldenrod, the asters, the smell of fallen acorns, the sulphurs are nothing more than momentary configurations of energy. The total amount of energy in the universe, some physicists calculate, is zero.

This whole September afternoon is a leaking illusion. None of it is real at all. No more real than a dream of butterflies, or a butterfly's dream of me. They're not playing, and there's no delight in what they're not doing. No will at work, no dance, no form, no consciousness, no idea, not even wind, dry grass, or goldenrod, or asters, not the mown field or cattails, not the other side of the fence, and not the sultry air of autumn because September is a fiction too.

The neuroscientists are wrong. None of this is there at all. I can see it's not there, like an image in a mirror.

Whatever is happening, it is not this. And it's big.

Notes from October

The oaks are finally dropping their leaves in droves. They and the beeches always hold out the longest, and so October, especially near the end, is gold and copper here. They're marcescent trees, meaning some of their leaves hang on well into snow season and even spring, when the great re-awakening unfolds and the old leaves are evidence that everything's returning, not spontaneously generating.

This year the red maple beside the driveway burst into flame a couple of weeks later than the usual September schedule. Every fall it goes up in a great tree conflagration over a week or two, then casts off all its scarlet leaves at once, usually in leaf-stripping wind and rain. Brown and gold carpets appear on lawns up and down Route 9. The birches dropped leaves at the usual steady pace that begins in September and lasts into November, and the deck is disappearing under their brown and yellow litter. The first trees to get naked are the ash trees, in September. Come to think of it they're the last to cover up in May, too, which might imply something about their libido. Probably not, that's arboreal anthropomorphism. Still, they're beautiful, plain and simple, and apparently needing more sleep than the rest.

The orb-weaving spider who moved in under the deck rail during August has curled up there and hardly moves any more. The conifer seed bugs are finding their way into the warmth of the house. I toss them out before somebody tries to kill them and causes a piney stink.

The birds in this particular autumn have been unusually sparse. In some Octobers we fill the feeders twice a day, but this year even the blue jays have shown up only occasionally to pilfer morsels from the cats' dish. A hundred years ago our clearing on the hillside was a cow pasture, and now it's enclosed by hefty pines, hemlocks and hardwoods, so our dooryard doesn't usually harbor a large avian diversity anyway. Mostly chickadees flitting from tree to tree and blue jays bullying them off every perch. A few red-breasted nuthatches have turned up, but squads of mourning doves that often patrol the firs have this fall been absent. A barred owl haunted the woods all summer, asking the other ghosts *who cooks for you?* all night, but he hasn't been heard since the eclipse. A few downy woodpeckers. Different sparrows, tufted titmice appearing and disappearing like foreign tourists. Crows overhead. One chilly morning what looked like a bear cub came barreling out of an oak tree and flapped across the driveway. It turned out to be a turkey.

A few juncos showed up in mid-October, hopping around on the ground and in the lower branches like tiny horizontal pogo sticks. Normally they blow through for a week or ten days going south and then again in late March headed north. But this particular fall there have been just that handful for a day or two. Maybe the warm weather in early October encouraged them to forage off the beaten paths. Still, you'd think the ever-slanting sunlight would tell them the tale of imminent cold.

We don't rake leaves because we need all the dirt-making material we can get. So usually I mow them to create a sort of mulch I hope will decompose under melting spring snow and reinforce our ledgy slopes. Next week chopped-up maple, oak and birch leaves will be corrugating the grassy parts of the yard. Next year's firewood is cut, split, stacked permanently covered beside the Shed. Life goes on, and the seasons, and everything else.

Healing Charms

Unprecedented cheerfulness erupted on our lawn, such as it is, in May one year and despite emotional headaches of our own that summer, gathered momentum right into the middle of September. We were beset, I mean, with an unusual abundance of heal-all and then a tremendous grove of eyebright.

The lawn gets the qualifier "such as it is" because, not to put too fine a point on it, the word "lawn" is a euphemism for the area around our house that is not overrun by birch and fir saplings and has a variety of grass species and dandelions growing with more and less success over certain swaths. The soil is made of crumbling rusty ledge and a typical northern New England crust of leaf-loam. Much of the year the surrounding pines, oaks, maples, poplars, hemlocks, cedars and beeches confine the yard largely to shadows, and hair-cap moss has colonized the margins where in a lighter climate you might hope grass would grow.

Anyway, droves of heal-alls invaded the shadowiest parts of the lawn during that summer, more than I've ever seen before or since. Their square stems are mostly two to maybe four inches tall, throwing little purple flowers shaped like smiling lips directly out of the sides here and there so hardly any individual plant looks like it's in full flower. They brightened up even the north lawn, which gets only morning Sun.

It was kind of disconcerting. What got into the heal-all?

I don't know. But I spent my grass-mowing sessions steering around the thickest outpourings just to preserve the charm of their color. When I got out the books to learn what,

177

exactly, was the silent attraction, it turned out that heal-all –
also called self-heal, woundwort and Prunella vulgaris – is a
long-known remedy for many ailments, especially mouth and
throat inflammations. In China it's called xia ku cao (not that
I knew that when I lived there years ago) and is thought to
help with dizziness and headaches and to improve vision. In
Europe it's been a base for poultices to stop bleeding from
open wounds. The Waldo County herb expert Tom Seymour
recounts that when he had dysentery as a boy, a decoction of
it made by his grandfather (who called it bumblebee weed)
saved his life.

After the onset of the heal-all, the ledgy, dry area beside
the Shed spawned its annual crop of eyebright. But that year,
what's usually a scattered band turned into a large grove in
one carpet-sized area. The little three- and four-inch plants
chased the normal stray hawkweeds and daisies, and even its
snapdragon cousins the butter-and-eggs, out of the way up
against the Shed and the foot of the woodpile.

The tiny eyebright corolla resembles common speedwell,
but the petals are pale, rich lavender with fine dark strokes:
Two little lobes pointing upward like a water droplet splash
over a lower lip of three notched lobes. When you get down
on their level you seem to be looking through strange
miniature trees partway along the back road to Oz. The grove
by the Shed might be a forest on another world.

It seems to be called eyebright because in olden times
infusions of it were used to remedy eye inflammations and
sties and to relieve eye strain. There are also indications it
might alleviate a cold, sore throat or allergy. The genus name,
Euphrasia, appears to share roots with Euphrosyne, one of the
ancient Greek Graces, who was an apparition of the joyful
aspect of Aphrodite. Whatever that means.

For us, as it happened, this was a summer of finding a way through some mottled emotional shadows of our own. The eyes can't be cured without attention to the head, some ancient saying goes, and those tiny cool-colored lavender and purple blossoms were little lawn charms for the mind. A biotic incantation of composure, like sophrosyne talking daylight, if you could just see them from the right angle.

Not really, you know. The woods don't care, as the wilderness guides warn their nature-loving clients. On the other hand, a clear view of sunlight streaming in through a grove of trees can be a moment by moment deliverance even when you're under the weather. The heal-all and the eyebright, I mean.

Late Bloomers

The youth culture, I'm afraid, left me behind. Not that I didn't practice it hard myself. Thirty years ago I bounced around – indelicately, as it were – on dance floors and wailed on electric guitars for dozens, sometimes hundreds of better bouncers than me, scoffed at organized religion, fell hard for every girl who smiled at me, and disdained small birds. Like every other kid who ever lived, I was a May-June slam-dance summer riot creature with wild-madder energy.

Slowly I wised up. Or something. Unfortunately, wising up is a drawback in the twenty-first century because we are obsessed with spring. If we weren't, the Viagra-Cialis industry would not do as well as it does. To the youth go the spoils. After that it's all downhill.

If you let it, I mean. Take the flora along my driveway, for example. In May and June comes the youth explosion. Starflowers, hawkweeds, raspberry, bluets, violets, ground ivy, wild roses, chokecherry, shadbush and crabapple blossoms, red osier dogwood umbels, little Canada mayflowers under the trees, wild strawberry, yarrow, rough-fruited cinquefoil (more perfect yellow petals do not exist in nature), wood sorrel, speedwell, and ineradicable outbreaks of dandelion.

About the beginning of July everything seems to lay back a moment, as if spent. Then it reconstitutes when the wild carrot, hemlock parsleys (or caraway, or whatever those white-crowned flowers by the mailbox are), bladder campion, evening primrose, St. Johnswort and nightshade, not to mention goldenrods, kick into rhythm.

By August and September the youth movement is gone and we stop thinking of flowers and start noticing fallen leaves. Beautiful, but smelling of winter. Here in the Western world we do not like to be reminded of winter. Its unstoppability.

But hold on. "Objects are concealed from our view, not so much because they are out of the course of our visual ray as because we do not bring our minds to bear on them," Thoreau, a man of no small wisdom it seems to me, observed of autumn.

Is there life after youth?

As late as the first week of October, the wall hawkweed, while not exactly in bunches, is nevertheless scattered all over the lawn. Clusters of New England asters, three feet high with gorgeous purple rays, grow along the driveway right where the cinquefoil appeared in June. Near the road among the defiant bands of hemlock parsleys (or whatever they are) are evening primroses four feet high with rich, bright-yellow unfurlings. There's late Queen Anne's lace, the last of the fading goldenrod. Some kind of skullcap with beechlike leaves and tube-shaped violet flowers grows right near the gravel. Down the embankment, clutches of pearly everlasting. Beside the woodpile, butter-and-eggs toadflax, tiny euphrasia, heal-alls looking deep-purple healthier than they did in July, and in the grass some little stray wood sorrel, late bloomers.

This is not welterous May and its single-minded reproductive roar. But it's a kind of fecundity that sees past its own growth and even, I have to say, beyond its own winter. There is, I happen to know from experience, a tiny flower called shepherd's purse, with little heart-shaped pods, that outlasts snowfalls too thin to survive the remnants of the Sun and thrives well into November and even December.

In the house, my old Gibson acoustic guitar sits alertly on its stand, ready to hand when the blues or the urge for goin' strike, stuff the kids don't recognize. My touch, though unprofessional, is defter than it was on stage at the Great Northeast Music Hall ten thousand springs ago. The chickadees bouncing around the bird feeder make me laugh out loud, and my wife, beyond competing with the cinquefoil, I fall for every time she walks through the kitchen.

Familiarity Breeds Content

All over the outside of everywhere in the middle of fall are the scavenging harvestmen, also known as daddy long-legs.

No one minds them at our house, the way some of us who are not me mind spiders. The main thing, I think, is that while most spiders look like they'd tear your face off and gnash it down if they were only a little bigger, daddy long-legs don't look the least bit fearsome. They amble around on these huge stilts acting like they're more curious than anything else. I was told when very young – and I imagine most everybody else learned the same folklore – that daddy long-legs don't bite, which I'm pretty sure made me feel well-disposed toward them.

It turns out this is true – they don't bite humans. Like spiders, they're arachnids, not insects, and have eight legs. But they're a different order, Opiliones, while spiders are of the order Araneae. (Ticks and mites are arachnids, too, but of the order Acarina.)

Hardly any spiders bite humans, either, by the way, and with a few unusual exceptions do no harm even when they do give a tiny frightened nip with their side-to-side jaws, or chelicerae. But the daddy long-legs lack fangs or venom, and they're prowling for unvigilant sowbugs, other small insects, mites, newly dead worms, even spiders, to eat. Some of them even nibble decaying plants and fungi.

Their long, thready legs are as important as they look. In addition to carrying their little bodies around (they actually do have two sections, like spiders, but the joint between the sections is so fat that harvestmen look like they're all head), the legs have olfactory and breathing organs. They also have stink glands under the first and second pairs, sort of like arachnid skunks, and some of them apparently use the little appendages called pedipalps, around their mouths, to mix an acrid-smelling secretion with saliva and throw it at predators. Nasty crafty.

The second pair of legs is the longest and most important. They're used like antennae to feel out the ground for things to eat. They can lose one of the first, third or fourth sets of legs and hobble on, even though lost legs don't regenerate, but damage to one of the second pair apparently is usually fatal. Interestingly, while their mating procedure starts off as basically a surprise attack by the male, once the brief copulatory embrace is underway, the couple gently stroke each other with those long legs.

There's something relaxed, familiar and domesticated about daddy long-legs. In Maine we most commonly see the Eastern harvestman (Leiobunum nigropalpi) and the brown harvestman (Leiobunum verrucosum). They scoot around the wood pile, along the railing of the deck and over the garden plants with a kind of leisurely arachnid grace. Maybe it seems graceful because I've never seen them eating or throwing spit at predators.

I've never seen them gather at night, either. But apparently they sometimes on cold nights group in huge numbers in a protected place like the side of a building with their legs interlaced in "a nightmarish hairball," as one field guide puts it. No one knows exactly why they do this. Maybe for warmth. Maybe for community purposes, which is kind of, well, touching when you daydream about it a little bit.

They're usually abundant around our house in the fall. Most of them do not survive winter, but the eggs are pushed into soil, moss or rotten wood, and another generation ambles out each summer, relieves us of some of our bugs, and helps give the backyard the familiar shape of fall again.

The Arachnids of October

By the latter part of October the araneids in the brush have mostly packed up for winter. I mean the big black and yellow garden spiders who all summer long construct big symmetrical orb webs in the grass and asters, and catch everything from gnats to airplanes, or dragonflies anyway.

By mid-October most everybody who figures to survive frosts and to overwinter is settling deep in the grass, or deeper, to hibernate. Others who don't hibernate might find their way to warmer places, like kitchens and door frames that are likely to harbor winter food items such as flies. Or so it usually goes.

The black and yellow garden spiders (Argiope aurantia) live only one summer, according to the books, and in October they've mostly finished binding up packets of eggs in the grass that will wait for winter to pass and then hatch out the next generation in April and May.

In milder falls, the spider populations overall – at least in their haunts that I haunt – can continue to thrive well after the usual September peak. On one late-October walk around the loop of the Unity park, I casually surveyed the metal benches just to see who might be toughing it out. One tiny fellow standing on the bare seat appeared to be sunning himself. It takes a few minutes for your eye to cross over into the miniature dimensions, and down there I spotted an even smaller spider, maybe a sixteenth of an inch, tending a thin network of web under the bench back. In fact, the place was still crawling with spiders. So to speak.

In the summer there are so many spiders that there's always one within about three feet of you no matter where you are. You hardly notice them because humans and spiders live in different planes or currents of the universe. That October afternoon, with my transparent arachnological eyeball, I walked along to the green chain-link fence around the basketball court. Inside the fence, another world.

In the breeze, long strands of silk waved from the linktops like fishing lines in the ocean. They were so fine they glistened in the eye only when just the right angle of light bounced in from the October west.

On the links of the fence were coils of fine silk, delicate to a human eye but probably like barbed wire to a gnat. Among the coils were more spiders, none with bodies more than about an eighth of an inch long. A few were sunning on top of the steel posts. Or my eye would pick up mini-movement in the links, where what I guessed were long-jawed orb weavers (family Tetragnathidae), long-bodied with long legs extending front and back, tended their nets upside down. A tiny jumping spider (Salticidae) with a hairy bulldoglike body ran and stopped, ran and stopped along the steel rail. In the photo later you could see his two big middle eyes peering curiously out from between two smaller eyes.

Along the fencetop and on the bench at least fourteen different species of spiders were still at work far into fall. In the coils ran long ones with tan-colored bodies, maybe three-sixteenths of an inch from head to butt. Some were smaller yet, with round dark abdomens and black cephalothoraxes (or heads). On top of one post was a crab spider (Thomisidae), who holds its front two legs like a crab's claws. This one was yellow and longish, a white-banded crab spider I think, though there are so many different kinds of spiders that identifying them is more like divination for amateurs like me. Around one hundred seventy-five thousand species of spiders are thought to be crawling the Earth. About forty-two thousand of them have been named. Our local experts estimate about six hundred eighty species live in Maine.

I watched the little crab spider sun for ten or fifteen seconds, then leaned over to take a picture, when pop! he flew off on the breeze by sending out a line of silk for a sail. Now I'd never actually seen this happen before, though I've read that this is how spiders fly. In fact, many spiderlings first leave the nest by sending out a strand of silk and letting the wind take them to their fortunes. Huge bands of "ballooning" spiders have been reported by ships far out to sea.

A little while later, off the front gate another spider, no idea what family even, also popped onto the breeze, and this fellow I watched float up and down for fifteen or twenty seconds over the grass.

Spiders fly off in the sky on strands of silk, and backyard naturalists throw their own lines underneath the benches and among the chain-link coils and find tough survivors. There are worlds within worlds. Sometimes they cross over.

Spider Food

A few days before Halloween, I was innocently washing up a few dishes at the sink and looking out the window at rain and the October blitz of juncos hopping around in the leaves. Cute, cheerful, industrious little fellows with slate-gray backs.

There was an odd flicker of movement in the upper left corner of the window. Uplifting my eyes from the sink, they fell upon a cobweb, and struggling upside down in it was a Western conifer seed bug. These guys invade the house every October and November to get out of the cold. They started showing up here ten or twelve years ago, apparently as climate-change immigrants from out west. They fly around like disabled Cessnas crashing into things and people's heads, and when they get scared, they nip. Not bad, but enough so you feel it. I usually put them outside.

This bug was in for something more horrible than October cold and rain, though. The owner of the cobweb, a house spider, scooted down the web and started working silk near the bug's legs. The conifer seed bug was four or five times as big as the spider. When the house spider approached, the bug struggled and tried to fend off the spider with its second, longer leg. The spider quickly lashed silk near the bug's foot and then ran back along the cobweb.

In a few seconds it returned, dodging the bug's kicking leg, made more quick lashings with deft movements of its front and second sets of legs, then dashed back. It ran back up the web, apparently tying off strands of silk paid out for the leg-tying. Sometimes it tied the strand in one spot, sometimes it made a semicircuit to several places where it worked for a few seconds, and then it ran back to the bug. The bug writhed futilely, kicking at the spider, but the spider quick fastened a bit of silk around the end of the leg and made its way back up the web to tie it off.

This went on for quite a while. The spider tied the legs down one strand of silk at a time, until first the longer kicking leg and then the smaller foreleg were both more or less shackled to the web.

At this point I left the scene for about two minutes to see what the cat had knocked over. When I returned, the conifer seed bug was no longer struggling, and there was a strong, moldy-pinelike stink in the kitchen, a smelly secretion the bug gives off in self-defense. The spider, no doubt, with the bug's legs lashed fast to the web, had run up and sunk the fangs in its side-to-side jaws (or chelicerae) into the bug and injected it with paralyzing venom. The stink defense didn't work.

The spider then retreated to the corner of the window. I assume it stayed there until the bug was completely paralyzed. Then it would start to eat.

The next day the conifer seed bug was hanging upside down farther up the web. Spiders of the Theridiidae family, like this house spider and the widow spiders, do not tear apart their prey, as some other spiders do. Instead they make an incision in the victim's body, into which they spew enzymes that digest tissue. The spider's stomach then acts like a pump, sucking the digested material into the spider's mouth and down its gut.

The spider ingests only soft material its body can absorb. Any hard particles that do not get pre-digested (especially among the spiders that first tear their prey apart and then soften it up with secretions) are filtered by hair around the spider's mouth and by platelets in the pharynx. Strange as it may sound, after a meal the spider washes up by cleaning the filtered debris from its mouth and hair.

The house spider probably got a number of meals out of the monstrous bug. Spiders by and large eat only living tissue. Or at any rate, things they kill themselves. An arachnologist told me it's not known how long the bug might live after receiving the paralyzing bite. I once watched a goldenrod crab spider muckle onto the face of a bee and hold it like that, sucking the insides out of its head for more than an hour, and thought that looked like a horrible way to die. This conifer seed bug, or at any rate its corpse, provided feasts to this house spider for three days, until one morning the hollowed-out body had been cut loose from the web and was lying on the window sill.

Even a few minutes of being eaten alive by a house spider must be like eternal hell to a bug. And worse if it lived on helpless for an hour, or a day.

Anyway, the juncos were still about the yard after the spider finished with the bug, bopping around in the leaves and eating, thank goodness, mostly seeds.

Halloween

By the end of October, the long decline toward winter has ceased being an autumn flourish and started to look inevitable. The world is literally dying.

The fields that turned from May-green to midsummer rust and then to hay are now expanses of stiff, dead grass and gray goldenrod. Milkweed pods have cracked and sent off wispy seed wraiths and are shriveling on the stalks.

The trees look like gray skeletons. Bony limbs and bare trunks stretch up hillsides and into untold miles of woods – you can't quite believe winter could undo so many so completely. But there they are by the thousands, sapless and naked, empty and deep at the same time, as if keeping something back. The firs and spruces seem clothed for the coming cold, but the maple, birch and ironwood leaves are strewn on the ground ready to return to dirt.

The leaves die by a process called senescence – which means growing old – brought on by declines in daylight and warmth. With less light, the tree manufactures less chlorophyll, which in summer makes the leaves green. Other chemicals also slow production, and cells between the base of the leaf and twig start to die. The dead cells thicken until they're brittle, and the leaf breaks off. A large maple tree can lose a quarter million leaves. When they're gone just the skeleton of limbs and branches remains, except for some whose marcescent leaves, like on oaks and beeches, cling to the twigs well into winter and beyond. No less lifeless, though.

The effect of this on your eye is a premonition of winter that turns into a chill in your spine. Its presence in the cycle bears an uncanny resemblance to death, or an idea we have of death, none of us having experienced it yet. Right at the end of October, when the woods and fields look this bare and lifeless, the ancient Celts saw the end of the year. The next day began their new year and in Christianity became All Saints Day. And that night before became "All hallow eve," which we've shortened to Halloween.

The Celts called it Samhain, and held a festival of the dead. It was thought that in the transition from the death of the old year to the birth of the new, the boundary between the otherworld, where the departed spirits dwell, and the natural world, where we live, thinned and broke down. The spirits of the dead could cross over to the world of the living, and vice versa, in that weird moment. To stave off whisperings that could harrow up your soul or freeze young blood, people in places like Scotland and Ireland impersonated the departed with masks and odd clothing. Large turnips were carved with faces as sentinels to scare off spirits. Later in North America, pumpkins worked even better.

By this time in the world of commerce and relaxed religion, All-hallow Eve has shriveled into a lark for children. But still, the natural ghosts of goldenrod and naked maples surround us like departed spirits, and there are times when you could almost think that just unseen in the woods there toward the cemetery, or trapped in the attic making faint rustling sounds, an apparition in the shape of a skeleton like a pile of dishes or a chandelier, with tongues of fire licking along its upper teeth and smoke rolling in its eye sockets had crossed into where it shouldn't be.

Or shouldn't it? Can't we know what the dead are keeping back? It happens every year, it's inevitable and all around us. You can see it there in the woods, that apparently go on forever.

Halloween Morning

It's cold in here. Dog-barks roll down through the woods and smoke in my skull.

I get out of bed, carry myself to the kitchen, and make coffee. Going every which way in the joints, I sit in front of the computer.

I spend much of the morning complaining to two friends. They seem to understand what I say. They are a dying breed, and they live hundreds of miles away. Why do they listen to this crap?

I stump around the kitchen rounding up my jacket and shoes. Outside it's chilly and overcast. The ash and poplar beside the driveway are gray skeletons. Blue jays are screeching about nothing in the bare branches.

I walk down the driveway. It is exactly one-tenth of a mile from the head of the driveway by the house to the mailbox on the road. On the way I think about at least six things I wish were going differently in my life.

At the road, a tractor-trailer truck roars past trying to blow me down the embankment. I keep my footing. I pull the newspaper out of its green tube box and two magazines and an AARP flier out of the mailbox. No one at our house ordered these magazines or reads them.

I walk like a pile of dishes back down the driveway with my hands shoved in my pockets and the papers tucked under my arm.

I stop near the brook and peer into the woods. The ground is carpeted with copper-colored oak and maple leaves. A trick of movement catches my eye sixty or seventy feet in among the bare trees. I stare between the trunks as far as I can. The forest floor is leaf-covered waves and troughs. Here and there a gray boulder. Not a bird. Not a squirrel. Not a deer. Nothing.

A thousand years ago, Wabanakis walked in these woods, talking in a language now irretrievably ancient. They saw the same maples, oaks, cedars, birches and fallen leaves. I do not see what they saw.

I walk briskly, for so slow a thing, back down the driveway toward the house. Two huge pines, a huge oak and a huge old red maple loom over everything on the right. Every morning for years and years they have loomed there.

The heating unit outside the house is humming. I hope it will last the winter.

Blue jays are picking at the bird feeder in the spruce. This feeder has not been disassembled by raccoons in weeks, that's a plus.

Inside, I drop the papers on the kitchen table. I take off my jacket and hang it on a chair. On the back step, blue jays are stealing morsels out of the cats' dish. Beautiful bright blue nasty-ass angels. Azure asuras. Loud-mouthed occidental tourists.

That's a little better. Despite being bullies the blue jays almost always have a good word.

I sit down in front of the computer. From on top of a stack of books, Edgar Allan Poe peers skeptically past my right shoulder.

Eureka! Words live.

A Decent Respect for Nature

The summer of 2014 was the hottest ever measured on Earth. Until 2015, anyway, which overall was hotter.

In central Maine, 2014 did not seem unusually warm, apart from a couple of spells in June and July. In fact, the National Oceanic and Atmospheric Administration maps indicated the high temperatures for the Northeast United States were near average for the summer of 2014. Some places you normally think of as being choking hot, like the Dakotas and Missouri area, were for much of that summer actually a bit cooler overall than usual. Things went along pretty much as usual.

On the other hand, the West was much hotter than the average of temperatures recorded since 1895.

NOAA says the worldwide land surface temperature for June to August 2014 was 1.64 degrees above the twentieth century average, the fifth-highest on record. The global ocean surface temperature was 1.13 degrees above the twentieth century average, the highest on record to that date for June to August; the previous record in 2009 was 1.06 degrees above the twentieth century average.

A University of Hawaii study found that 2014 saw the highest global mean sea surface temperatures ever recorded. Up to then, at least.

Even though it's soothing to your conscience to think this is all a kind of random tumble of temperatures that the Earth experiences all the time, the fact is, it's not. The general climate – and now the particular weather – is undergoing disruptions that have not been business as usual over the past few hundred thousand years, according to the climatologists.

Measurements of our own hyped-up slashing and burning practices over the past roughly two hundred years correspond directly to measurements of unsettling changes.

It's not like no one saw it coming. In the late 1700s there was a widespread perception that a general, unhealthy divorce of humans from nature was taking place. By the middle of the 1800s, coal smoke in cities was literally choking the life out of people.

A push for conservation emerged in the United States by the late 1800s, partly because of incredible leaps in scientific understanding that helped lead to a new recognition of our situation in nature. In the humanities we call the American version of this recognition the philosophy of Transcendentalism. To say it more plainly, it was a re-invention of the way we look at the woods.

Henry David Thoreau, Ralph Waldo Emerson and their cohorts realized that the idea of nature as a foe to be defeated is essentially a negation of ourselves – self-destructive, in other words. We are an element of nature. It informs us, and we inform it.

Thoreau, in particular, recognized that we live inescapably in a borderland between the necessities of civilization and the necessities of wild nature. Scientific method, for Thoreau, was a way of seeing into the layers of reality in our borderland.

"Let us not underrate the value of a fact," he wrote; "it will one day flower in a truth."

That is a key sentence. The physical world is a prism of truth and, moreover, beauty. It could be apprehended through scientific method, in Thoreau's description, or as a personal experience, in Emerson's description: "Standing on the bare ground ... I see all; the currents of the Universal Being circulate through me; I am part or parcel of God."

Maybe, almost two centuries later, we would not express it quite this way. But on the other hand, many people feel a sort of reverence when they go to the woods to camp, fish, hunt or climb a mountain. We go there to put ourselves in the way of that feeling. It can get very strange, sometimes, when sunlight strikes a certain slant down through the trees, a blue jay whines in just a certain crack of time, or the wind rattles oak leaves.

In that moment you feel like you've touched a spot of time where you and the naked beauty of nature are informing each other equally.

That can be a moment of transparent uplifting beauty, or it can be a moment of terror. A moment in which you remember, as I do, something like walking to work in a small city in the Balkans on cold winter mornings, with so much soupy, sulfur-smelling coal smoke in the air that within ten minutes you were short of breath. And realizing suddenly that this choking smoke has been pouring into the air worldwide from stoves, cars, factories and conflagrations for centuries.

The ancient Greeks' story of Actaeon is one of those minor myths no one pays much attention to. He was a virile young guy who, like his friends, enjoyed hunting with his dogs and riding roughshod over the countryside. One day he paused to rest in some pine woods and heard a stream running nearby, and voices. He went nearer and saw, bathing naked in a clear pool, Artemis and her handmaidens.

He was awestruck – there before him was the spirit of the woods, pristine, naked, unforgivingly beautiful.

Artemis turned and saw him looking. Angered by the violation, she turned him into a deer. He ran off into the woods and was chased by his own dogs who hunted him down and tore him to pieces.

Before he saw nature in her true form, Actaeon lived in a sort of day to day, unthinking oblivion, tearing things up, hunting things down, and throwing away the rest. When he stumbled upon nature unclothed, he was suddenly face to face not only with its beauty but also with his own violent violation of it.

It didn't matter that he came upon Artemis by accident. The woods, as outdoorspeople persistently warn, have no concern for you personally.

As science peels back layer after layer of reality, it also reveals layer upon layer of startling beauty. Sometimes it's a conventional kind of sensory beauty, like the Hubble Space Telescope photos; sometimes it's an abstract kind of mathematical beauty, like the incredible finding that the amount of energy in a particle of matter is equal to the mass of the particle multiplied by the speed of light *squared*: $e=mc^2$.

Sometimes we find layers that are not beautiful at all. Sometimes they're terrible and horrifying.

Gee, we didn't know we were poisoning the air, water and Earth. Or, even if we did, we didn't mean to.

Doesn't matter to Artemis. And the warming oceans are already starting to dog us.

November in Troy and Florida

In the middle of a mild November, Jack (age: now purchases beer legally) and I flew to Jacksonville, Florida, to attend my niece's wedding. My nomadic impulses have subsided in recent years, and I guess I forgot the world beyond Maine looks different. The irregular hills and ruts of Maine live deep in me, and Florida's gauzy, half-drunk summer landscape – in the middle of November – plastered my mind's eye like an immense dew.

November is not our most cherished month, at least not here in the accelerating seasonal rounds of the spruce-northern-hardwood forest area in the Troy woods. It's the harbinger of winter, after all. It's a pause, like a held breath, just before the deep cold.

Your eyes get used to November looking like November – brown, gray and copper. Maple, birch, ash and popple by midmonth turn into skeletons. They leave a rough, brown, dead-acorn-smelling rug of leaves on the woods floor. Milkweed, aster and goldenrod stalks are lace-frail cadavers. Corn stubble and pumpkin vines are bent old men. Cattails, which were rich brown in August, are frayed, corroded sticks. Red winterberries glare out of bare tangles.

Crows, chickadees and nuthatches hang around the empty hardwoods and in spruces and hemlocks that are less like life and more like dark green blankets. The wild turkeys march through single file from time to time, and the blue jays seem bright against the copper oak leaves. But the juncos who hopped around in the leaves like exuberant fifth-graders during October are gone, and so are the warblers, most of the sparrows, and the hummingbirds who split in September.

The purple martins see it coming even earlier, and vacate in August.

Somehow this sense of an impending ending that gathers like storm clouds carries a certain clear, sober comfort: I've seen these gray-brown woods teetering on the still point of the turning world many times, and taken this deep breath ahead of the great white wall of winter. And I – or someone, anyway – will see it all again. November's great stillness is a blessed evening, you could say.

So my eye could not make sense of Florida's lightning colors. The big-finned palms and vines, the moss hanging off giant live oaks were like flakes of botanical flame to my New England-centric eye. Fruit was still ripening on my brother's lemon tree. In November? Not only were his jalapeno peppers still reddening, but his basil, thyme and coriander (which simply doesn't survive at any time at our house) were thriving in the little garden of his low-slung, one-story, hurricane-proof house with window sills a foot from ground level. Cardinals, some kind of scrawny blue jay and exotic sparrows visited the garden; what might have been a red-tailed hawk monitored things from high up. Watch out for alligators and water moccasins, and sure enough I saw a brown-backed snake slither through a patch of unmown grass. By 10 a.m. it was 75 degrees, humid and blurry.

To me, this all seemed like a riotous lack of seasonal decorum. Everything was drunkenly angering for life when it should have been soberly reflecting on the cusp of winterfall and the end of everything.

But the gold side to these unseasonal green sides: Jack seemed to fit right in. He had his shorts and T-shirts ready to go when we got there. He sank his toes in my brother's shag-carpetlike lawn. He drank beer easily with my brothers, which (since we're from Maine, after all) did not take me by surprise. But then during the wedding reception he suddenly had a highball glass in his hand, which turned out to contain a stiff dose of vodka. This glass with twizzle stick and lime disoriented me more than ever.

But when I paused and reflected, I recollected times when all of nature, no matter where it was or when, synchronized with my imagination and the flatlands of elsewhere were as inspiring as the betangled and rutted Maine woods. In those days the whole world was a teeming green home, whether it was the gray trees of central Maine or the lavender-flowered garden of a cozy Florida flood-plain house. When Jack was a little boy, we walked up through winter flowers to the top of the Pnyx hill in Athens and looked out toward the Acropolis with just that feeling of flame and morning. That was as intoxicating to me as the immense dew of Florida is to Jack.

But now, at the end of autumn, the backyard in Troy still and always looks exactly like Thanksgiving. I am happy to report this.

Turkey Day

Turkey day is family day. People flock home, wherever they conceive that to be, every fourth Thursday of November. For us older thankers, memories of turkeys past always hatch out again too, reborn from some undiscovered country to whose bourn all travelers return year after year.

I wonder how many turkeys our family has eaten since my son Jack joined us twentysomething years ago. The farm-raised ones, I mean, not the wild turkeys which in recent decades have been proliferating, according to the accounts and to how often they slow Bonnie and me down while they cross a road, or wend the driveway single file into the woods.

Turkeys, like most birds, it turns out, are quite family oriented. A book that has stayed with me, *Illumination in the Flatwoods*, describes Joe Hutto's experience saving a few orphans from oblivion. In his wooded North Florida neighborhood (about the time Jack came into the world, this was) a forestry effort was under way to improve quail habitat by cutting down pine trees and eliminating hardwood transition areas. Good for the quail, but bad for the turkeys. Their nests were getting destroyed.

So after a conversation with a local farmer, Hutto found on his doorstep one May morning a clutch of live turkey eggs. He took them in and makeshift incubated them. The memorable part of the story is the little turkey poults hatching out. They don't just break free of the eggshells, wander around dazed, then grow up. They look around for Mom or Dad.

In his description, the newborns are frightened until they spot and make eye contact with an adult protector. This is called "imprinting." So in the barn, each one would see him peeking over the tabletop and run to his face, stare into his eyes, then nuzzle up against him and fall happily asleep. After that, their poulthood included peeping happily whenever he appeared, running to him and crowding around him. He'd lay down with them and they'd push their fuzzy little beaky faces into him, nestle down, and sleep. He spent the summer and fall taking them for walks, protecting them from snakes, weasels and hawks, and generally being their parent. For at least two years he was apparently the poults' idea of a family.

You have to think that in a turkey's mind, this is not a terribly complicated notion. Powerful with turkey emotions and instincts, no doubt, but not complicated. In humans, on the other hand, a webwork of memories, feelings, hopes, thoughts and other inner experiences that turkeys (presumably) do not have is integral to our sense of "family." Including, weirdly, eating turkeys in November.

It's complicated. Jack in his teenage years for a while wrote an occasional newspaper column called Nature Notes, and one of them, the most accomplished that I remember, went like this:

"It was a cold February day, and we had just come home from town. My five-year-old nephew, Zachary, was with us. He was excited to have 'a sleepover' with us at our house in Troy. We gathered up the groceries and Zachary's things from the car, and started to head inside. Then Zachary stopped, staring curiously down the driveway. He pointed and said, 'What's that?' They were turkeys, or wild turkeys to be exact.

"There were several of them. A few were making their way through the deep snow, a couple perched in a nearby tree. I was amazed when a couple of them took off flying. In fact, turkeys can fly up to sixty miles per hour, and as far as about a mile per flight. It was not unusual to see so many turkeys together all in the same place. They require lots of mature hardwoods, more specifically the nut producing species (like oak or beech), along with pines. This makes Maine (and our backyard) a prime location for turkeys.

"Early in Maine's history, Eastern wild turkeys flourished in York and Cumberland counties. By 1880, though, much of southern Maine had been cleared of trees and 90 percent was made up of farmland, so the wild turkey population plummeted. This, and unrestricted hunting were thought to be the two major factors.

"Later, as farming declined, the woods regrew. Now, farmland in those areas covers only about 15 percent, and attempts were made after World War II to reintroduce wild turkeys. In 1977 the efforts succeeded. In the 1980s more turkeys were brought to Waldo and Hancock counties, and [in 2006] the state's wild turkey population is estimated to be around forty thousand birds."

Jack gave up writing in favor of less contemplative activities, but this little achievement of course has lived close to the surface of my memory for years. Every November I remember it. I devour it, actually. Quite thankfully. It's a little oviary of all that is, or ever was, or will be.

November's Gray Dissolution

Before the snow in November, you can see right through the trees into the dead of winter and beyond it.

Early on in the month one year, I set out on an overcast, wind-bitten afternoon to walk the railroad tracks along the shore of Unity Pond. I wanted to see what the buttonbush brush looks like at this time of year. It was a gray, skeletal blur, like everything else. A little finer in the twigs than chokecherry, maybe. But on the edge of winter it comes to the same thing.

The bog between the tracks and the mouth of Sandy Stream was expectedly withered and brown. It was the exact natural reflection of William Faulkner's phrase "November's gray dissolution," which when I first read it forty years ago rang like a voice off Mount Sinai. It's echoed back every deer-hunting month since, as reliable as frost in October or the geese flapping and racing on before the snow.

Faulkner's story "The Bear" is about hunting, I was thinking while I calculated each irregular step from railroad tie to railroad tie, and part of the ancient tradition is getting hammered to ward off the chill, among other things. This reminded me that I had, when you got down to the bone of it, actually put myself in danger by walking exposed along these tracks in my gray autumn jacket. There was a clear shot at me with a deer rifle from the other side of the bog, and there's a sense in which it would be entirely my fault if somebody's optical equipment transformed the line of my slightly bent gait into horizontal brown fur.

A drug like alcohol can encourage this phenomenon, of course, but you don't have to be drunk for it to happen.

Objective physical reality and your experience of it unify in your mind, and the biochemistry that makes up your brain has ways of reshaping reality that are to some extent under your control according to your inner strengths and weaknesses. It's possible for the mind of a completely well-meaning person with too much eagerness, too little inner discipline and a rifle to turn a human figure into an ungulate figure. As, tragically, we know.

So foreseeing the possibility, however remote, of becoming a party to my own sudden passage into the next world, I turned around before I reached the trestle bridge, got in the car and ambled back out along Kanokalus Road, which runs right through the middle of a cemetery.

November's dissolution does not get any grayer than this. Its beauty is astounding. Lines of maples, birches and ash who have gone bare for the long sleep. Apple trees with dark fruits but no leaves. Milkweed feathers and fraying cattails, leaf detritus, goldenrod ghosts, the shells of Queen Anne's lace, staghorn sumac naked except for small pyramids of dry drupes, dead grass, all of it reddish brown. Towering overhead, luminous yellow tamaracks. The sparrows of fall, the Canada geese in loose low-altitude chevrons. Even at midday the Sun drops only in windless dappling on the ground. All that stays is dying, and all that lives is getting out, the song says.

It's a kind of magnificent desolation, to lift a phrase once applied to the surface of the Moon, that telescopes your mind. The unstacked firewood from backyard to backyard is like a thousand other unfinished projects teetering on the edge of too late. Winter is not now, yet it will come.

Here and there along the roadside, through gray, bare, bony tangles, winterberries remain like red candle flames. Ilex verticillata, the arborists call the bush, black alder to the rest of us. Overwintering birds, raccoons and mice will get the seeds when the better foraging has itself gone south. The fruits turn human stomachs, but in the mind's eye the startling red berries run tunnels through the gray twists and turns of deep brush, and transform November, there in the far invisible post-frozen distance, into the rosy underpresence of spring. The readiness is all.

Late November

Just before a recent snowfall, I stopped along the walk I take most mornings and saw four ducks paddling around on the beaver pond.

The pond was slate-gray and flat, in that hunter's stillness November balances on. The air is chilled, but not yet wintry. The trees are bare. Their branches are gray and skeletal, and ragged white clouds knot in dark blue sky. Hardly a breath of wind.

I crossed the road and climbed up the short, steep bank of dead grass. Over white-green moss and juniper, under cedars and tattered spruces, I made my way to the edge of the pond, which is held back by the outcropping of ledge where I stood and a makeshift barrier of deadwood and leaves which is leaking. A hundred feet across the pond is a beaver dome of piled and interlaced sticks. By the far shore were the ducks. They looked like black ducks.

I watched them glide around on the shale-like water. From time to time one stuck his head under and after a pause came up spluttering and spraying beads of cold water around. They meandered in the direction of the beaver dome.

Suddenly there was splashing and wingbeats, and they were airborne, rising like seaplanes. The strange thing about this is how they all spring together – not one after the other, or three following one who panicked, but all at the same instant. They flapped almost in unison and climbed smoothly over the water and the beaver dome, then the frost-crusted hayfield beyond.

About the time they crossed the shoreline, a great blue heron arose like an apparition from the reeds the other side of the beaver house. It was shaped like an assembly of joints, with sharp head and long neck, immense pointed wings and slate-blue sticklike body. It had the angles of a pterodactyl and the beauties dinosaurs lacked, and it was, amazingly, totally silent.

Its wings stroked slowly and powerfully, moving without pressure, almost, over the wet leaves in the autumn chill. It seemed to float through the air, headed westerly behind the ducks.

Weeks earlier in October, as I was walking up the driveway near the house, a motion over the brook in the fir woods twicked the corner of my eye. I hesitated and turned, and saw a gray-blue winged shape rise from the brook, waft up through the trees, and vanish. It was noiseless as the woods. It had the size and shape of a heron, but how could a bird that large navigate through hemlocks and pines? I wondered if I hadn't seen a woodland ghost leak from a crack between two seconds.

The heron over the pond also ascended in complete November silence. The pond surface was undisturbed, and all I heard for some moments was water trickling out through the stick dam and across rocks into the gully by the road. Everything had paused, as if taking one last breath before winter, and then was quietly gone.

The Frontier

The day before a November snowstorm, a few vestiges of summer dangled like bits of grass and twigs in autumn's last spider webs. A lone yellow hawkweed, contracted against the cold, looked up out of the grass by the gravel walk. A little viney beast with tiny white blossoms and heart-shaped pods grew near it – shepherd's purse, it was. There were dull orange marcescent oak leaves. Stiff willow-herb. Winterberry branches heavy with red berries, like a galaxy spun from seed. A murder of crows in the topmost branches of empty maples. Up above them, two undulating V's of Canada geese honking in the cloud-strewn distance and flying due south. Lake Winnecook was as flat and gray as slate.

This was late in November. That night in a kitchen window two brown-colored spiders were hunkered down at the center of their geometric webs. These two orb weavers might have lived so long because of the unusual warm that fall, but I didn't know. They could not survive the coming snow, I didn't think.

They rode the billows and bounces of their webs together in the November gusts. One was constructed in taut, carefully measured rectangles radiating from the center. The other looked miskempt, with trapezoids loosely lashed to rough triangles. This spider was probably older than the other, less disposed to neatness. They were hunkered down in the centers, waiting for bugs that would never come. The silk was very tough against the wind which batted them up and down, and they clung there waiting.

They probably did not have long to live. Soon they would starve or succumb to the cold. But if they lasted through the night, they would dutifully build again. They were like two old Chinese poets banished at the end of their lives to the northern frontier and gazing northward into places so bleak it's almost unimaginable. Cold, rolling, rocky grassland in the dark, with nothing beyond but more dark and grassland and strews of boulders and somewhere mountains. No family, no town, no tomorrow. Only vast, empty winter, in the end.

Eight or nine inches of snow came and covered the gravel and willow-herb and goldenrod skeletons where the banded argiopes perished long ago in October frost. Whether the two old poets in the window survived, I don't know. I didn't see any new webs after the storm. The shepherd's purse lived through two more snows. The oaks were almost stripped. Cold and more snow were coming. Winter is vast in northern China, and in Maine.

Sources of Information

This book comprises essays, not scholarship. It should never be cited as a reference for factual information. The author not being a scientist, the scientific information here is neither firsthand nor authoritative. No list of sources is included because no systematic method of documenting sources was ever devised. Information was gleaned from what has amounted probably to thousands of books, magazine articles, scholarly papers and websites, each of which was carefully vetted for its authoritative integrity by the author (who holds a doctorate and a commendation for excellence in graduate research, just not in a science). In some cases, experts in Maine or elsewhere were consulted by email or phone for clarification. Any errors are due to the author's misreading or mistranscribing. Most often directly quoted is Henry David Thoreau, and those brief passages came from the following books: *Excursions* (Peter Smith, 1975); *Selected Journals of Henry David Thoreau* (Carl Bode, editor, New American Library, 1980); *The Journal: 1837-1861* (Damion Searls, editor, New York Review Books, 2009); *The Maine Woods* (Princeton University Press, 1983); and *Walden* (Princeton University Press, 1973).

About the Author

Dana Wilde lives in Troy, Maine, with his wife, Bonnie Woellner. He received a bachelor's degree in English from the University of Southern Maine and master's and doctoral degrees in English from Binghamton University in New York; taught at the American University in Bulgaria, Unity College in Maine, the University of Maine at Augusta and the University of Maine in Orono, among others; served three appointments as a Fulbright Scholar at Xiamen, Lanzhou and Fudan Universities in China and the University of the Witwatersrand in Johannesburg, South Africa; and has been an editor, a rock and roll musician, and a basketball coach, among many other things. His books include *Nebulae: A Backyard Cosmography*, *The Other End of the Driveway* and *The Big Picture*, and his writings have appeared in publications such as *Pluto: New Horizons for a Lost Horizon*, *The Magazine of Fantasy & Science Fiction*, *Mystics Quarterly*, *The Café Review*, *Exquisite Corpse*, *Detritus*, *The North American Review*, *Island Journal*, *Maine Boats Homes & Harbors*, and many others, and, as of the summer of 2016, in his Off Radar and Backyard Naturalist columns in the *Kennebec Journal* and *Morning Sentinel* newspapers.